FRANK GASCOIGNE HEATH

1873 – 1936

A BIOGRAPHY

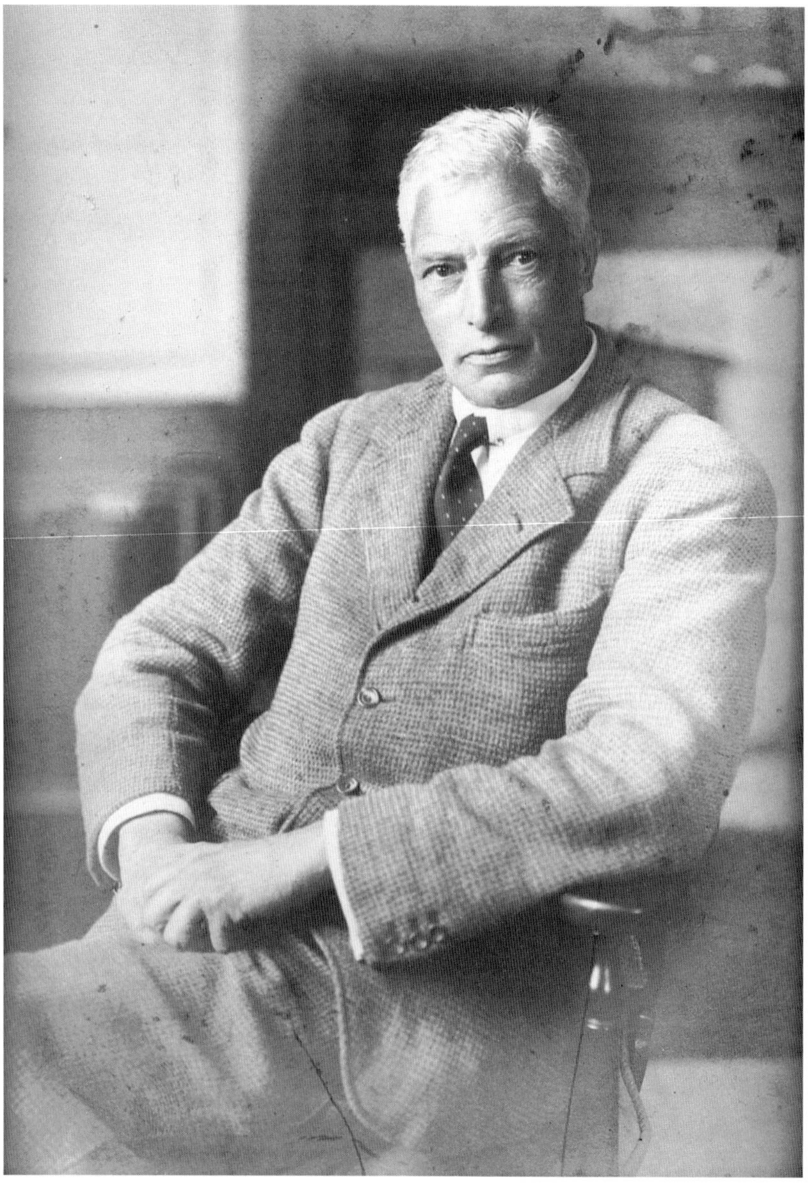

Frank Gascoigne Heath - 1930

FRANK GASCOIGNE HEATH

AND HIS "NEWLYN SCHOOL" FRIENDS AT LAMORNA

HUGH BEDFORD

To Mrs. Bosch,

with best wishes

Jane & Hugh Bedford

July 1998.

In memory of Tony Heath who gave me many recollections of his father's life; without his help and inspiration this book could not have been written.

Acknowledgements: I would like to thank the following for all their help, information and advice:

Hazel Berriman of Royal Cornwall Museum, Truro; Colin Bird; Robert Bruce-Gardner and William Clarke of the Courtauld Institute of Art; Gabriel Carruthers; Jack Collins; Caroline Fox; Estelle Fox; Keith Gardiner; Peter Garnier; John George; Thomas Gibson Fine Art, London; Malcolm and Lisa Gray of Lamorna Cove Hotel; Melissa Hardie of Newlyn Art Gallery; Bobby Heath; Jonathan Holmes of Penzance & District Museum and Art Gallery; James Rawlin and Diana Kay of Phillips, London; Alex Kidson of Walker Art Gallery, Liverpool; Graham Bazley of W H Lane & Son, Penzance; Victoria Law of Richard Green, London; Grant Longman of Bushey Museum; Carol Tee of David Messum Fine Art; National Postal Museum; Mary Noble; Maryella Pigott; Margaret Powell; Royal Academy of Arts; Leonora Simpson; Sotheby's, London; Jan Swinglehurst; Olwen Tarrant of Royal Institute of Oil Painters; Enid Truman; Ann Turner; Reg Watkiss; Michael Williams; Witt Library, Courtauld Institute of Art; Jean Goodman.

I would especially like to thank Robert Cotton for his photography, John Beresford for most generously supplying his map of Lamorna, Rachel Wallis for her word processing skills and my wife, Jane, for all her help in so many ways.

ISBN 0 9524087 0 8

Published by Hugh Bedford of PO Box 3, Teddington, Middlesex, TW11 0BT, to whom any enquiries should be made.

Printed by Clarendon Printers Limited, Beaconsfield, Bucks.

CONTENTS

INTRODUCTION

"The Newlyn School"

"...the applause has not been stinted and the Newlyn School can surely not complain of want of recognition." These words of gratitude from artist to critic were written by Stanhope Forbes in 1898. Ten years earlier, reference to the "Newlyn School" had first been publicly made and the same critic had said that "Newlyners are the most significant body of painters now in England." Throughout the 1890s the title "Newlyn School" was regularly and familiarly used for the group of artists who worked in this West Cornwall fishing village.

For a few years before 1888 the artists of Newlyn had seen themselves as a distinct group. "The RA this year may best be described as the 'triumph of Newlyn'", wrote Forbes in 1886 and in 1887 he proudly announces that "Newlyn has come off wonderfully".

Both Thomas Cooper Gotch and his future wife Caroline Yates, and Walter Langley and his first wife, are said to have visited Newlyn on more than one occasion some years before settling in the village. But there is no doubt that Walter Langley himself was the first settler, early in 1882. He was followed closely by his friend Edwin Harris. When Stanhope Forbes arrived early in 1884, from Brittany, he wrote home immediately that "Newlyn is a sort of English Concarneau and is the haunt of a great many painters."

Stanhope Forbes, especially, had taken as his inspiration, the French "plein air" realist

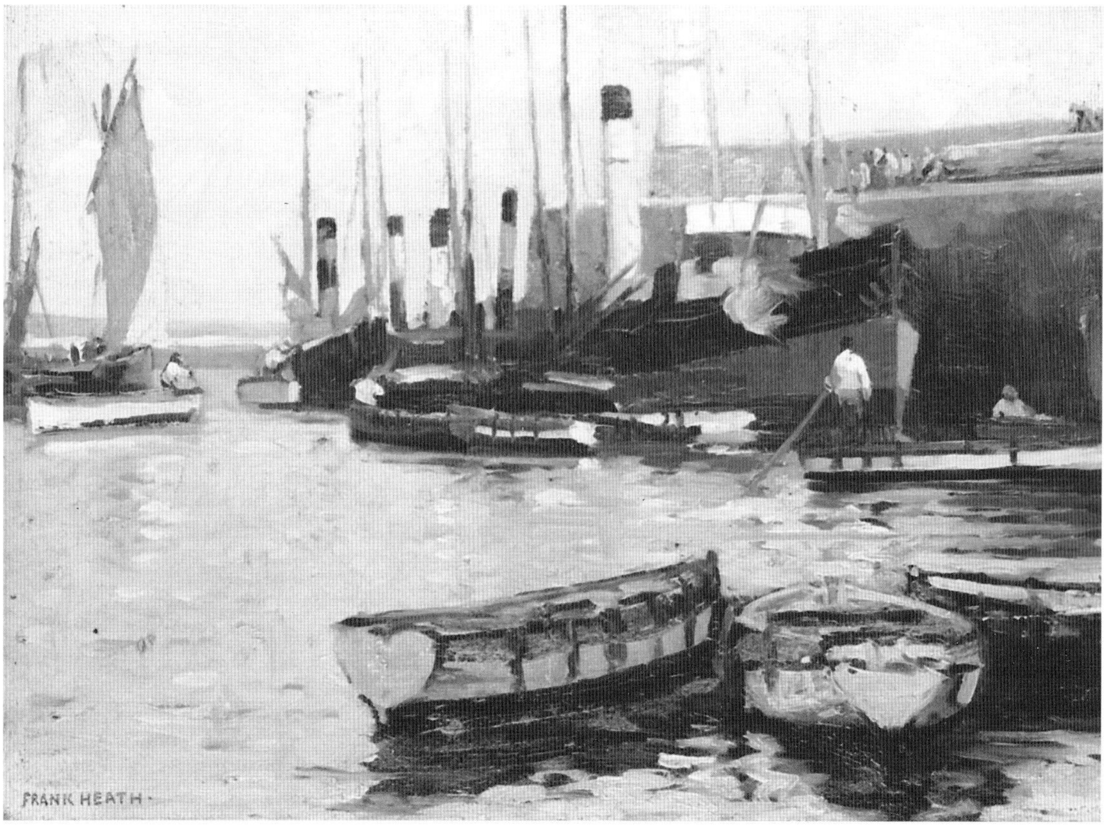

The Entrance to Newlyn Harbour ("the Gaps") by Frank Heath

painters and, in particular, the works of Jules Bastien-Lepage (1848-1884). During his short life Bastien-Lepage, with his sympathetic depiction of the life of simple working folk, made a lasting impression. It was this genre that Stanhope Forbes and his fellow painters carried forward to Newlyn in their pictures of the fisherfolk.

Of this first generation of Newlyn artists few really settled in the village. However, some of the principal ones did stay - Walter Langley, Thomas Cooper Gotch, Norman Garstin and Stanhope Forbes.

From the turn of the century a second generation of "Newlyn School" artists arrived, drawn, in particular, by the influence of Stanhope Forbes and the "School of Painting" that he had founded in Newlyn in 1899 with his wife, Elizabeth. Several of their followers and students made their homes in the beautiful valley of Lamorna, about three miles west of Newlyn and six miles from Lands End; these included Frank Gascoigne Heath.

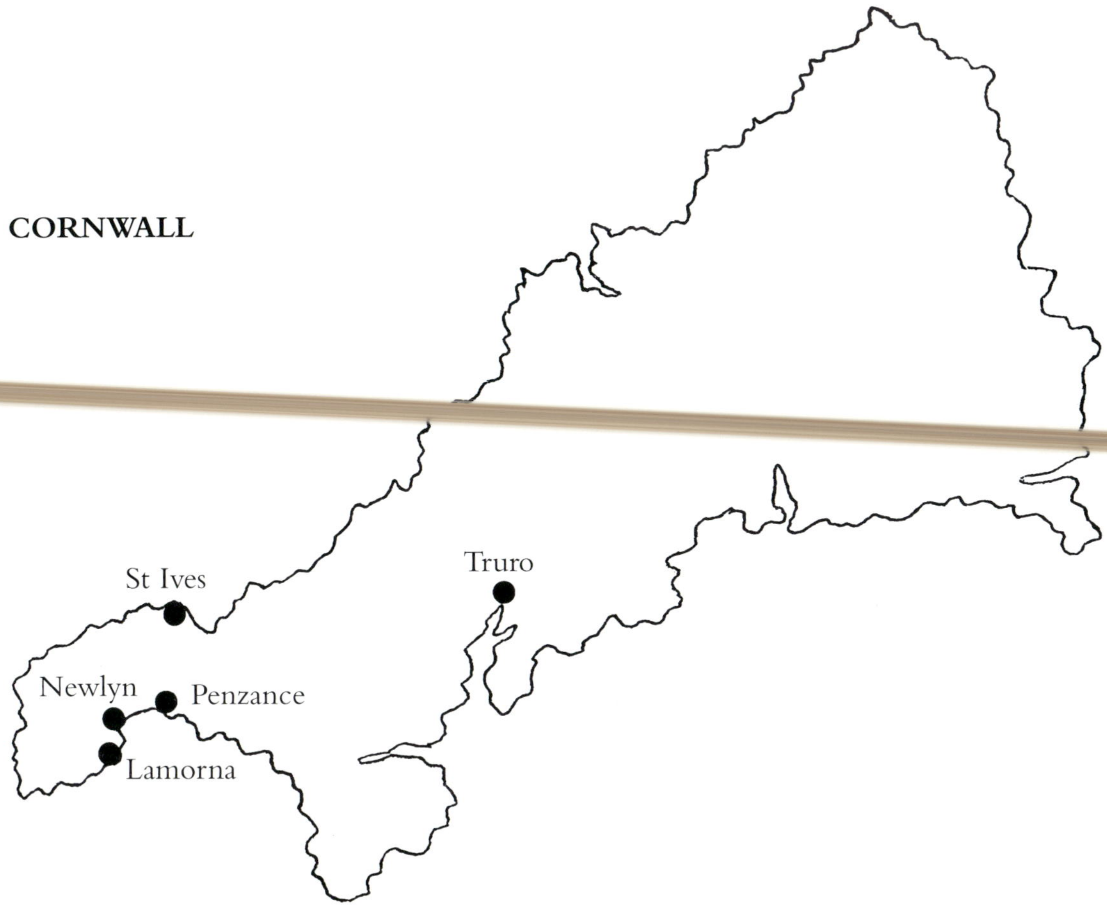

The Heath Family Tree

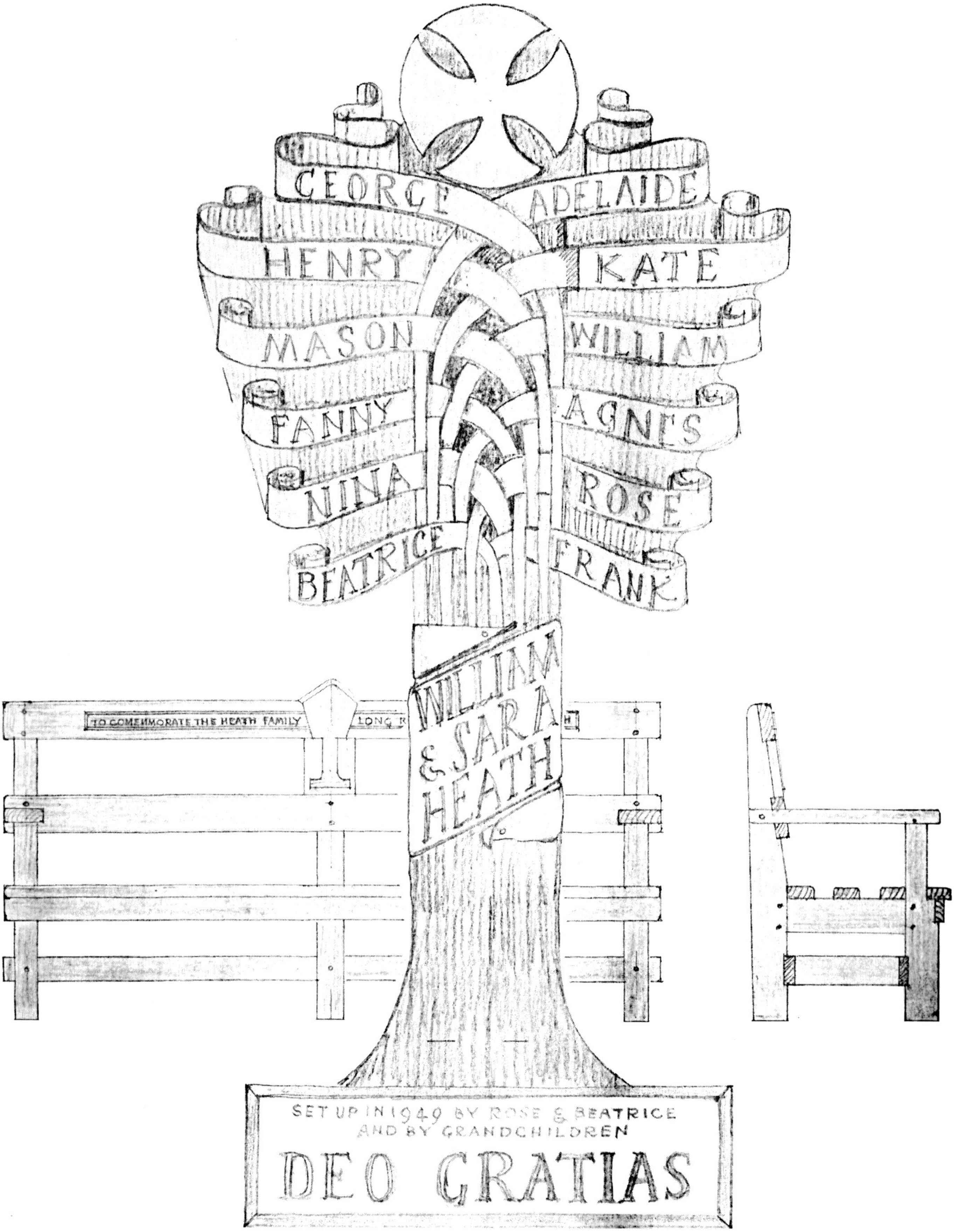

Chapter 1

HIS EARLY LIFE AND INFLUENCES

Frank Heath was born at the family home, "Woodlands" in Coulsdon, Surrey on 23 January 1873, the youngest of 12 children of William Henry Heath and Sara Blay. William Henry Heath (1833-1880), was Building Surveyor to the Bishopsgate Ward in the City of London. He married Sara Blay (from Kirkby Stephen, Westmoreland) at St Leonards Church, Foster Lane in the City in 1855.

The family tree opposite (created in bronze to commemorate the family and fixed to a garden seat in the churchyard of old Coulsdon Church) shows the names of William and Sara Heath's 12 children (5 boys and 7 girls, born between 1856 and 1873); all lived well into the 20th century. Frank's elder brothers trained and entered the learned professions of law and surveying, while 6 of the girls married. Adelaide, who was the eldest daughter and single, studied the piano in Leipzig and became a very good pianist.

At this stage it is worth mentioning two notable ancestors of the family from whom, no doubt, Frank inherited his artistic talents. James Heath and his son, Charles were both engravers of great skill and prestige in the early part of the 19th century. At that time there arose a "school" of interpretive engravers who were entrusted by Royal Academicians and other prominent artists of the day to make line engravings of their pictorial works for reproduction in books and journals; both James and Charles were part of this "school".

James Heath was born in 1757 and was apprenticed to a distinguished engraver, Joseph

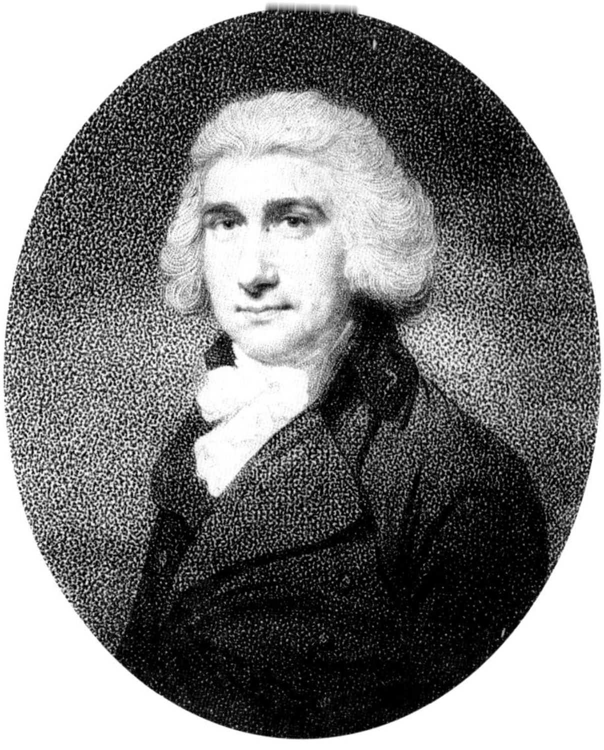

James Heath, 1757-1834
Historical Engraver to the King.

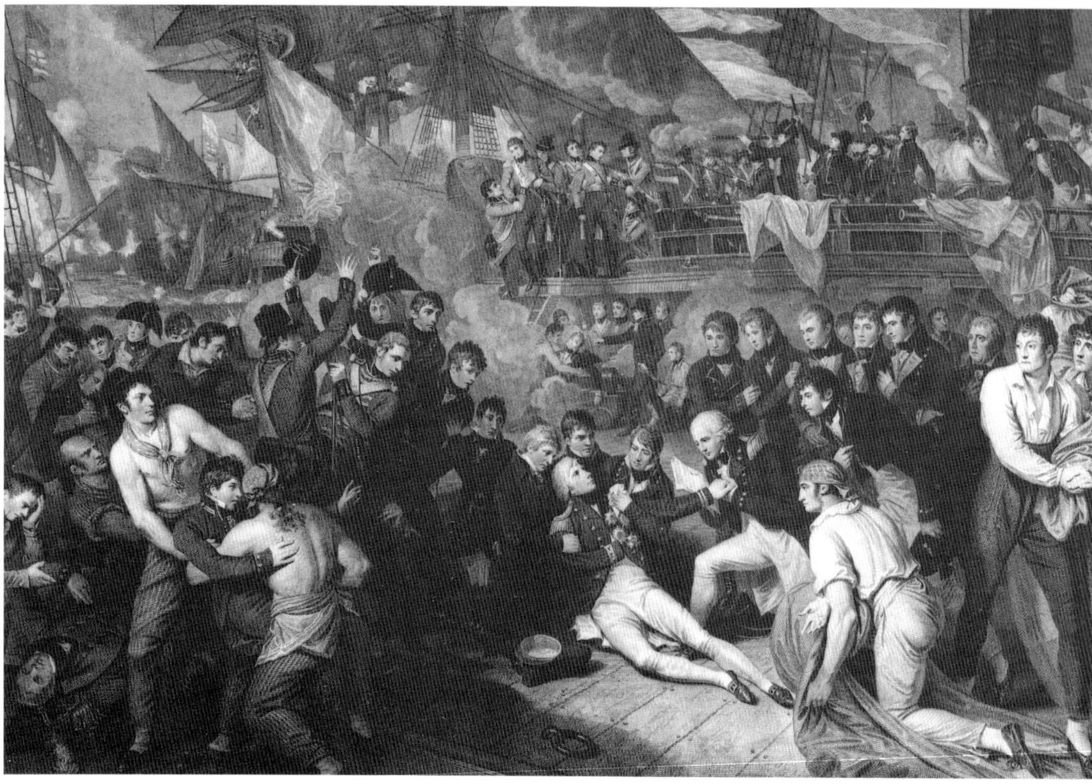

Engraving of "The Death of Lord Viscount Nelson" by James Heath after Benjamin West, PRA.

Collyer, in the City of London. Among his early works were portraits to illustrate the writings of Horace Walpole. As he became better known, he produced numerous engravings after designs by Thomas Stothard, RA, Robert Smirke, RA and other book illustrators. However, his major and best known works were large plates depicting historical scenes such as "The Death of Lord Viscount Nelson" after Benjamin West, PRA, "The Death of Major Pierson" after John Singleton Copley, RA and "The Gordon Riots of 1780" after Francis Wheatley RA.

James was elected Associate Engraver of the Royal Academy in 1781 and in 1784 received the appointment of Historical Engraver to King George III, continuing in that post under successive sovereigns until his death in 1834.

Charles Heath was born in 1785, the illegitimate son of James from whom he received his early instruction in engraving. An etched head done by him aged 6 is in the Print Room of the British Museum and he was, in many ways, more naturally gifted than his father. He achieved near perfection in his preparation of small plates for numerous popular editions of English classics; likewise, some of his portraits such as that of "Lady Peel" after Sir Thomas Lawrence attained great excellence. Early in his life he was made a Fellow of the Society of British Artists.

Because of the known quality of his work, Charles had the honour to be chosen to engrave the dies for the world's first adhesive postage stamps, issued in May 1840 – the penny black and twopenny blue. In the engraving of his stamp die, he worked from a number of line drawings made by Henry Corbould.

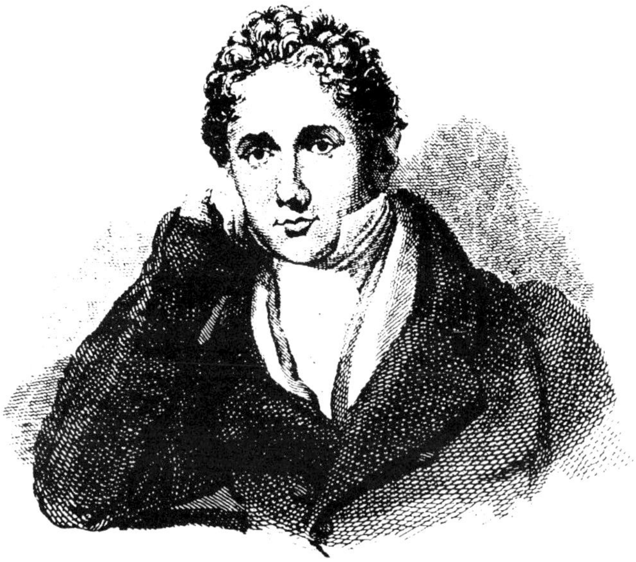

Charles Heath, 1785-1848 Master Engraver

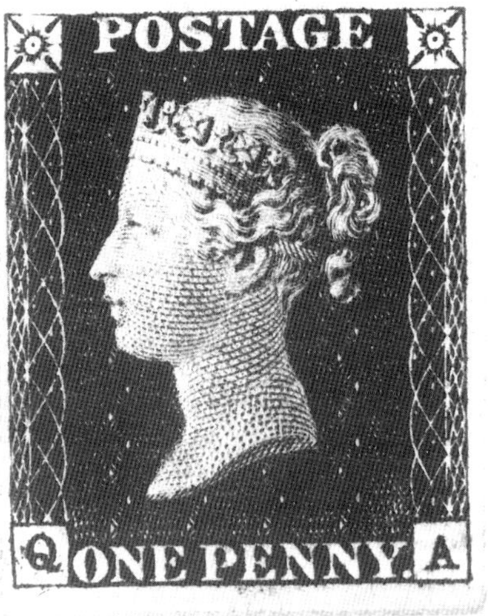

Penny Black

Now we move forward 40 years and return to the young boy Frank who was only 7 when his father died in 1880 and was brought up at "Woodlands" by his mother and elder sisters. He was educated locally and it was while at school that he first showed the artistic talent which was to lead him to art school and then to Cornwall. His mother, Sara, lived into her 80s and, in 1919, towards the end of her life, Frank Heath travelled up from Cornwall to visit her at Bexhill-on-Sea where she was living at the time (perhaps to be close to her daughter, Nina who was nearby.) While staying at Bexhill, Frank painted scenes of Pevensey, Rye and Bexhill.

As a child, Frank did not enjoy good health, suffering from chest problems. In order to try and help overcome these, it was decided that on leaving school he would go to sea to "toughen him up". It was arranged that he should be taken on as an apprentice to the Captain of a windjammer sailing to Australia. He would have been away for many months; it must have been quite an adventure and, one would imagine, an ordeal for him. He obviously suffered no after effects as he was sent off next on a climbing expedition in the Alps which appears to have completed the cure of his bronchial troubles.

On his return, Frank Heath decided to pursue his first love, which was painting. His early training as an artist began at South Kensington Art School; it continued at Croydon, Westminster, the Academy of Fine Arts in Antwerp, Belgium, and the Herkomer Art School at Bushey in Hertfordshire.

Frank Heath studied at the Academy of Fine Arts in Antwerp from 1895 to 1897 under Albrecht de Vriendt, the Principal of the Academy (from 1891-1900) and Pierre van Havermaet. De Vriendt was chiefly known as a painter of historic and religious scenes and the pictures, by Frank Heath, entitled "Below in the valley, there lies the world" (shown at the Liverpool Autumn Exhibition of 1907 - see over), and the interior of a church at Louvain, near Antwerp (see Plate 1), certainly reflect the influence of de Vriendt in his work and are so very different to his later "Cornish period". Pierre van Havermaet was best known for his painting of portraits. He taught for many years at the Academy, where one of his pupils, in 1886, had been Vincent van Gogh.

After Antwerp, Frank Heath returned to England to further his studies at Sir Hubert von Herkomer's Art School in Bushey, one of the major art schools of its day and often used as a form of "post-graduate" tuition.

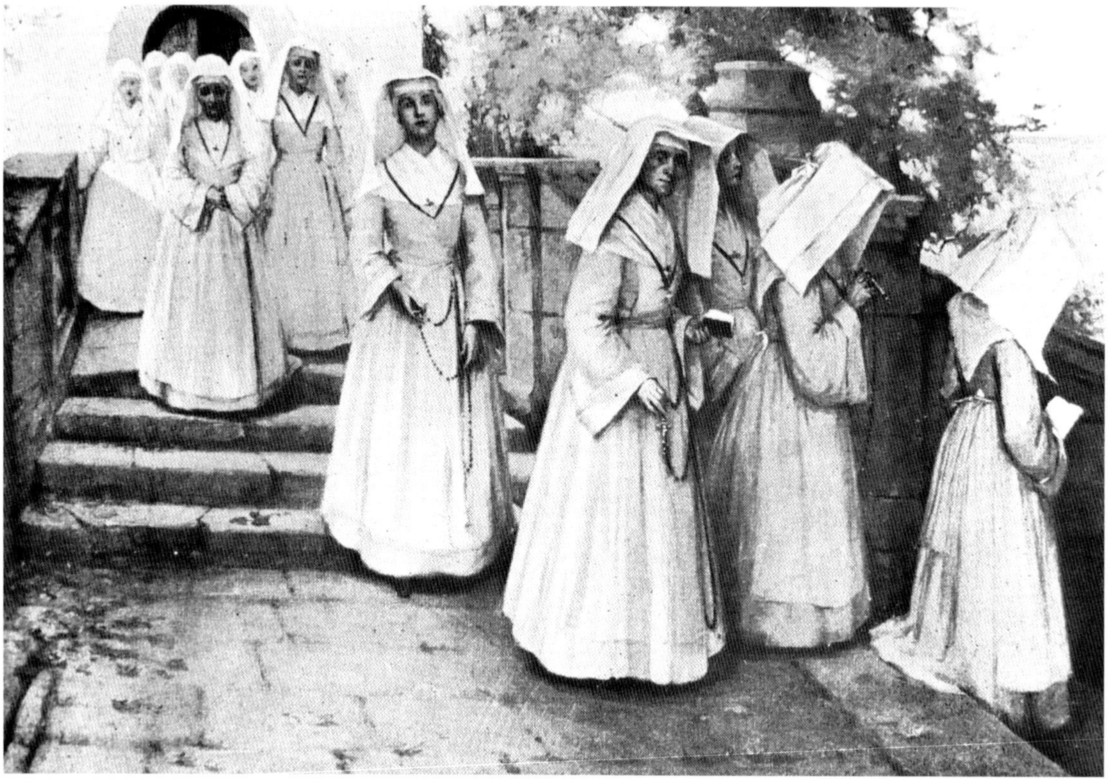

"Below in the valley, there lies the world" by Frank Heath

Herkomer was born in Bavaria in 1849 but came to England with his family when aged 8. From the later part of the 19th Century until his death in 1914, he was the foremost Society portrait painter; his subjects included Queen Victoria and numerous notable Victorians, and he was made a Royal Academician in 1890. However, amid his more strictly professional engagements, some of his best known major paintings like "Hard Times", "On Strike" and "Our Village" (see opposite) show a sympathy with the problems of the working-class and a realism that make them important documents of their lives.

It was in 1883 that Herkomer opened his Art School at Bushey with 25 pupils. The School soon developed until Herkomer was surrounded by a populous colony of 150 young men and women scattered about the village in cottages and studios, absorbed in their many sided interests - artistic, musical and social. The centre of this arts settlement was "Lululaund", the huge house and arts and crafts extravaganza, built for Herkomer between 1886-1894.

To be admitted to the School, candidates were required to send in a drawing, in charcoal, of a head done from nature. Upon such work, seen personally by Herkomer, they were admitted to the Preliminary Class. He set a very high standard and was progressive for the time in encouraging students to develop their own style.

The School became world famous and around 500-600 students attended over a span of 21 years. Amongst the well known artists whose success stemmed from the School were the Royal Academicians, Sir John Alfred Arnesby Brown (1866-1955) and Algernon Talmage (1871-1931), both of whom had later connections with St Ives, and Lucy Kemp-Welch (1869-1958) who purchased the School from Herkomer in 1904 and proceeded to

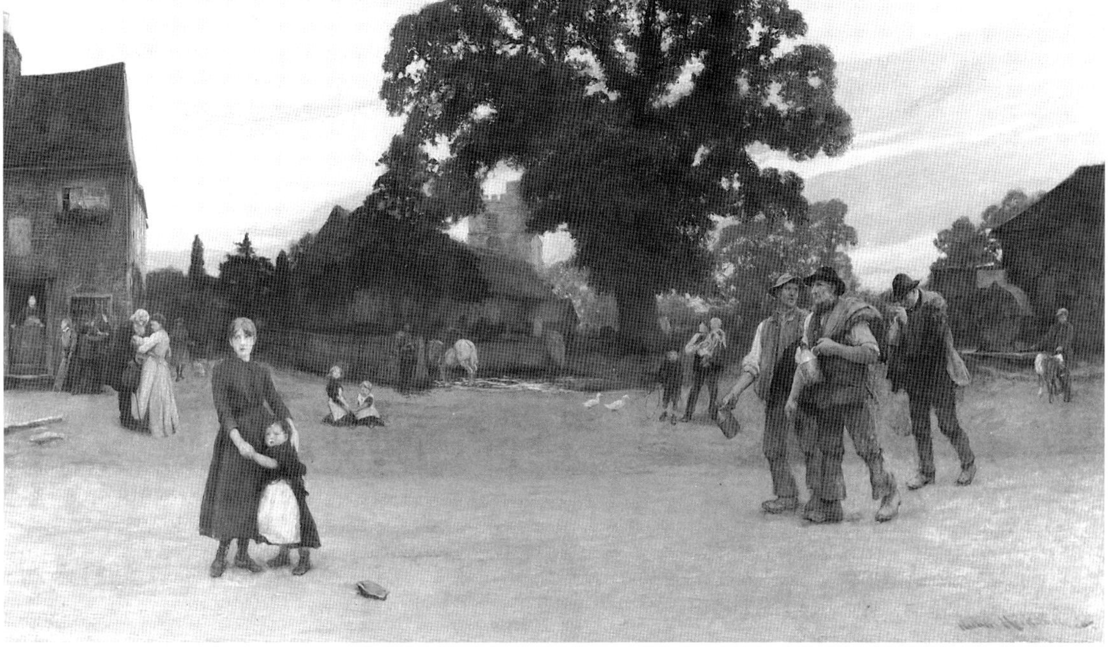

"Our Village" (Bushey, circa 1890) by Sir Hubert von Herkomer

run it herself. Charles Simpson studied there for a short period before settling in Newlyn.

Frank Heath joined the School in October 1897 and stayed for the full three year course. While studying there he was attached to the Chapel Studios and it is possible that he lodged with one of his older brothers, William and his wife, Laura who lived at Bushey. During his time there, he exhibited three works at the Society of Oil Painters (now the Royal Institute of Oil Painters) annual exhibition held at the Piccadilly Galleries in London.

1899	"A Study"	(priced at 10 gns)
1901	"An Interior"	(priced at 15 gns)
1901	"An English Lane"	(priced at 50 gns)

Herkomer's capacity for work was enormous, although he often also dragooned students into doing some of his artistic chores. He shared an interest in several other aspects of art and usually displayed amazing skill in each field that he took up. He trained himself in various forms of fine art printing, such as etching and it was perhaps from Herkomer that Frank Heath learnt this skill which he was able to put into practice while living at Lamorna. (See etching of Clapper Mill on page 42.)

After finishing at the Herkomer School, Frank Heath set off for Brittany, perhaps wanting a change from the formalized art teaching he had received over the preceding few years. It may also be that he wanted to be part of the informal groups of artists that had set up their easels and painted in the open air in Brittany: no doubt he had seen their work displayed at various exhibitions including the Royal Academy. One of the best known of these artists was Stanhope Forbes. While in Brittany the attractions of this style of painting obviously appealed to Frank Heath and on his return to England, he decided to travel to Newlyn to work with Stanhope Forbes.

It was early in the 1880s that several English artists who had furthered their studies in both Paris and Brittany "discovered" Newlyn. One of these was Stanhope Forbes, whose purpose, when he set off for Brittany in 1881, was to paint in the open air (or "plein air") rather than work entirely from a studio; he wanted to paint ordinary people in harmony with their surroundings. At that time in France, "plein air" artists were in the ascendant.

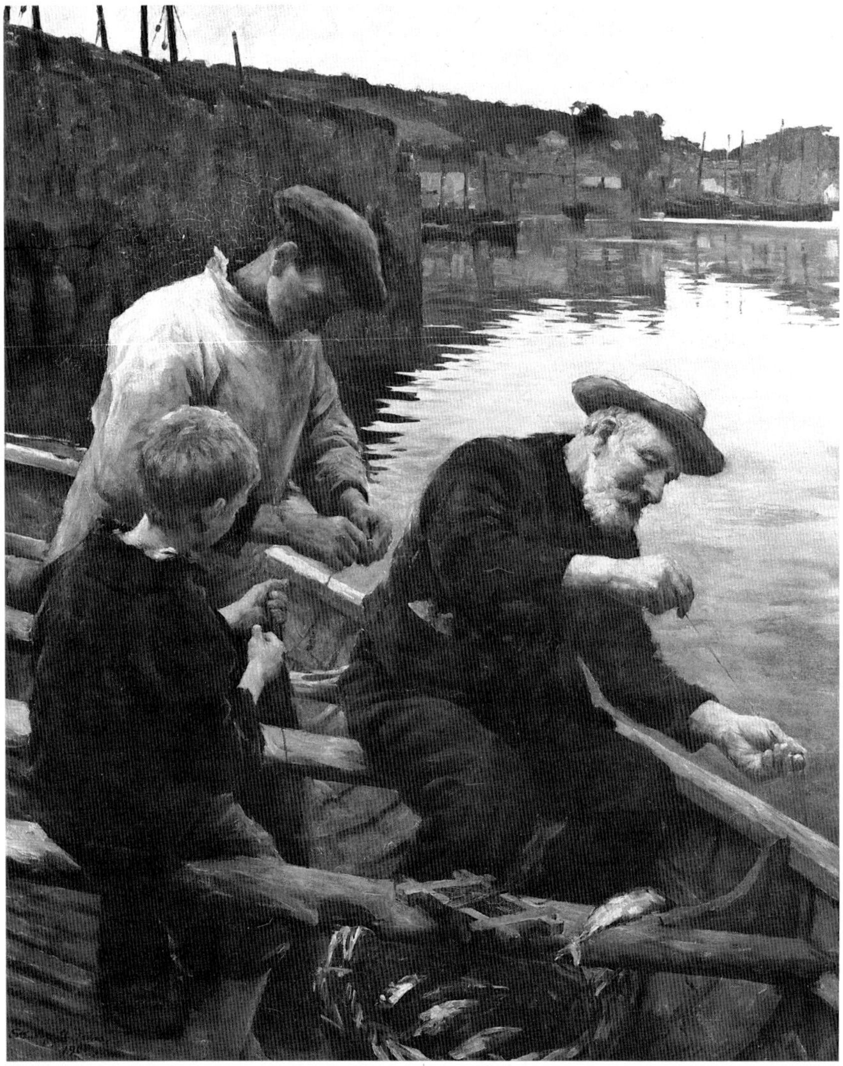

Newlyn 1906
by
Stanhope Forbes

Stanhope Forbes wrote "...under the spell of the genius Jean Francois Millet and the more recent Bastien-Lepage, most of us young students were turning our backs on great cities, forsaking the studios with their unvarying north light, to set up our easels in country districts where we could pose our models and attack our work, in sunshine or shadow, under the open sky."

In 1884 following another visit to Brittany, Stanhope Forbes took the train to

Falmouth to look for new sketching grounds. Moving west he settled in Newlyn; what appealed to him was not only the character of the village but also the number of artists already living and working there. Newlyn was perfectly suited to the artists' needs, with its mild climate and good light being favourable to painting in the open air, together with the picturesque occupations of the fisherfolk.

Stanhope Forbes was born in Dublin in 1857. He learnt to draw while at school at Dulwich College; after leaving school, he went on to study at the Lambeth School of Art, the Royal Academy Schools and in Paris. From 1884, when he made his home in Newlyn, until his death in 1947 aged 90, Stanhope Forbes's influence and reputation, not only in Cornwall, but also elsewhere was well earned. From 1885 onwards his great successes at the Royal Academy Summer Exhibition led to the wider recognition of the group of artists working at Newlyn. In 1886 he became a founder member of the New English Art Club (together with, amongst others, Thomas Cooper Gotch and Henry Scott Tuke). He was made a Royal Academician in 1910.

In the mid 1880s Stanhope Forbes met a young Canadian fellow artist in Newlyn, Elizabeth Armstrong, and they married in 1889. It was ten years later that they opened their School of Painting, "for the student who wishes to learn how seriously to study painting and drawing according to the recent developments in English Art". The school buildings consisted of three wooden studios set in a large wild garden on the hill slope in an area in the heart of Newlyn known as "The Meadow".

Every Saturday during term "The Crit" was held in one of the studios. This was a review of all the students' work, consisting mostly of sketches hung unsigned in order to achieve impartiality. "The Professor", as Forbes was called, would then come and pronounce on the work with all the students sitting in a semicircle behind him. One student, Ruth Alison (later to marry Charles Simpson and live at Lamorna), recorded how at her first "Crit" she "shook with fright when the Professor approached her work", since he had a reputation for being quite merciless on occasions. This time, however, he was very kind, saying that the pictures were very well drawn and done tenderly and carefully. On another occasion, however, her work was "slanged". Forbes commanded great respect at the School and Ruth recalled her delight when he returned from a period away: "I am so glad Mr Forbes is back, the whole atmosphere of the place is altered when he is here."

The school's formation marked the beginning of a new era in the artistic life of the village; its students were to be the nucleus of the second generation of Newlyn artists. Frank Heath travelled there in 1901/2 to work and study with Stanhope Forbes. He found lodgings at Trewarveneth Farm which stood at the top of Paul Hill on the outskirts of Newlyn, where he joined other artists living and working there. It was a great meeting place; Alfred Munnings was a frequent visitor and numerous excuses were made for parties. Stanhope and Elizabeth Forbes were living there before they moved in 1906 to "Higher Faugan", the house that they had built for themselves nearby and it is very likely that they recommended Trewarveneth to Frank Heath.

Elizabeth Forbes died in 1912. In 1915, Stanhope Forbes married Maudie Palmer, herself a painter and former pupil of the school. Over the years Frank Heath and "Stannie" became great friends and Maudie became godmother to Frank Heath's only son, Tony. Stanhope Forbes is buried in the churchyard at Sancreed.

It was while living at Trewarveneth that Frank Heath had his first pictures accepted by the Royal Academy for their Summer Exhibition - including in 1907 "Shoving Off" (Plate 4) and 1909 Cut Throat Euchre (Plate 6).

In addition to study at the Forbes' School, there was no lack of entertainment in the artistic circles of Newlyn. Parties and musical evenings were held at Trewarveneth and other houses; (Frank Heath and Stanhope Forbes would both have taken part in these, playing the violin or piano and cello, respectively.) Dances were organized by the students and in the summer picnics were held.

Stanhope and Elizabeth Forbes were succeeded at Trewarveneth by Thomas Cooper Gotch, his wife Caroline and their daughter Phyllis. It was while living at Trewarveneth that Phyllis set her sights at Frank Heath. Phyllis Gotch was a great extrovert. Laura Knight in her autobiography "Oil Paint and Grease Paint" wrote "... Phyllis Gotch would organize extraordinary parties. It was difficult to resist her persuasive powers; ... Phyllis announced that she had completed arrangements for a grand display - an evening party was to be given on Trewarveneth lawn - Phyllis and I were to be principals in a Grecian dance." On another occasion "... Phyllis took us by storm. This time we were to act, sing and dance in a hash-up of musical comedies which affair was to be held at the Church School Hall at Newlyn ... no one knew their parts - the pianist failed to turn up owing to a tiff. Frank Heath was called up from the audience to read the score, a brave show on his part - leaves of music kept dropping and the pencilled instructions were impossible to follow."

However, around this same time, Frank had met an attractive student studying at the Forbes' School, Jessica Doherty from Bandon, Co Cork. Jessica's father Richard Doherty was Agent to Lord Bandon's Irish estates and following a successful career handling these matters, he decided to retire and left Ireland to settle in England. At that time his son Ernest was graduating from Trinity College, Cambridge and was thinking about a career in mining. The family moved to Newlyn, bought "La Pietra" on Paul Hill and Ernest commuted to Camborne where he enrolled at the School of Mines. At the same time Jessica was keen to learn painting and, with the Forbes' School so close at hand, enrolled as a student.

Both Jessica and Phyllis were, at the time in their mid 20s while Frank was 10 years older and a tall, good looking bachelor. Eventually, it was Jessica who won Frank's heart and they were married at Paul Church on 30 March 1910.

Phyllis was also friendly with Ernest, Jessica's brother and shortly after Frank and Jessica's wedding, Ernest and Phyllis married. They went to live in South Africa where Ernest was employed as a mining engineer. Tragically, after only a few years, he contracted miner's phthisis and died in 1915. Phyllis returned with their baby daughter, Patsy, to live with her parents in Newlyn.

Meanwhile, after a honeymoon in Venice, Frank and Jessica had set up their first home at Osprey Cottage in Polperro and it was while they were there that their first two children were born, Aileen and Nancy. After two years at Polperro they decided to move back to West Cornwall and settle in Lamorna.

Chapter 2

LAMORNA

Lamorna, meaning in Cornish, "valley by the sea", is one of West Cornwall's most beautiful valleys. It lies snugly between the hills with a little river running softly as it hurries between the trees southwards to the cove and sea.

Flowers abound; especially in the spring with daffodils, bluebells and primroses. Cottages and houses, well sheltered from the elements, nestle along the banks of the river; building materials proved no problem - there was plenty of stone from the quarries and much well seasoned wood was washed up along the shore; this was used for some of the cottages one of which is named after a wrecked ship "The Oriental".

In contrast, the cove is harsh with, on either side, the cliffs rising to three hundred feet with huge granite rocks scattered everywhere - a reminder of times past and the quarries. Looking east from the cove one can see the headland of Carn Du - Black Point. Walking

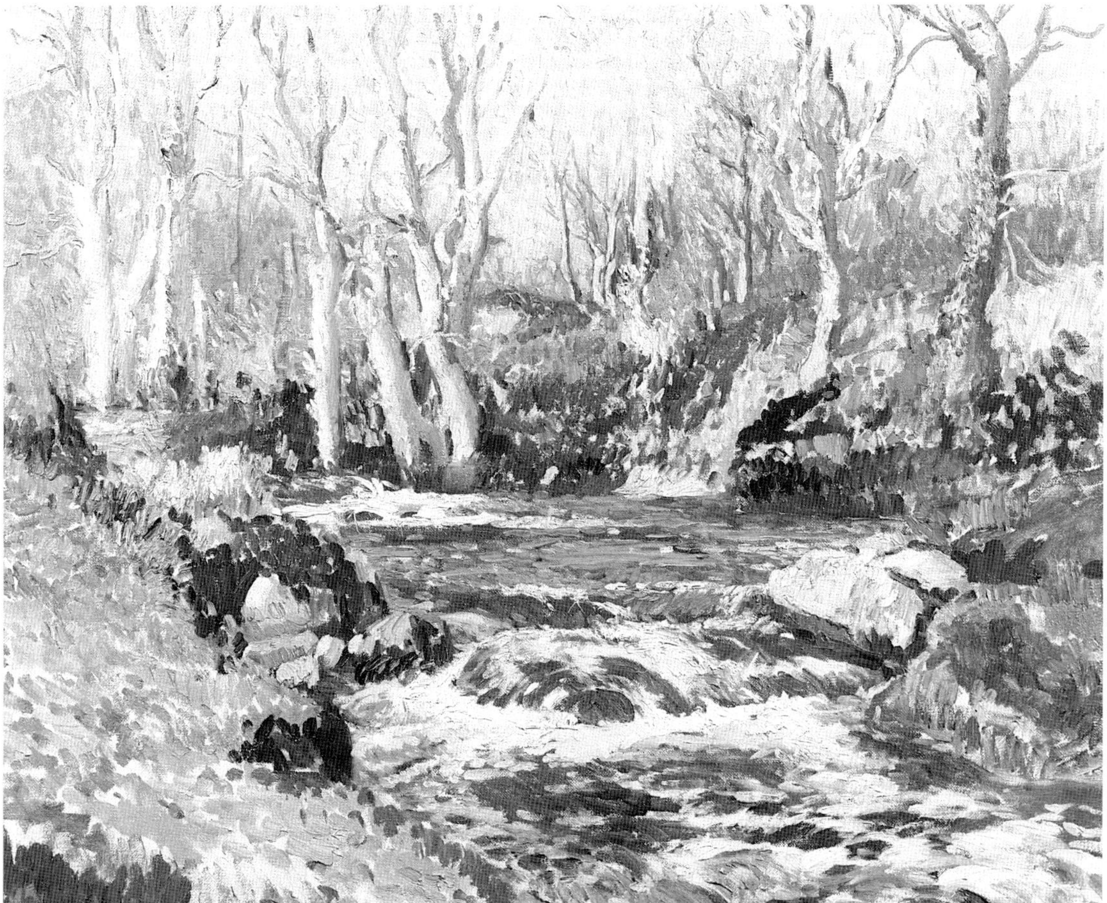

"Our little river at Lamorna" by S J (Lamorna) Birch

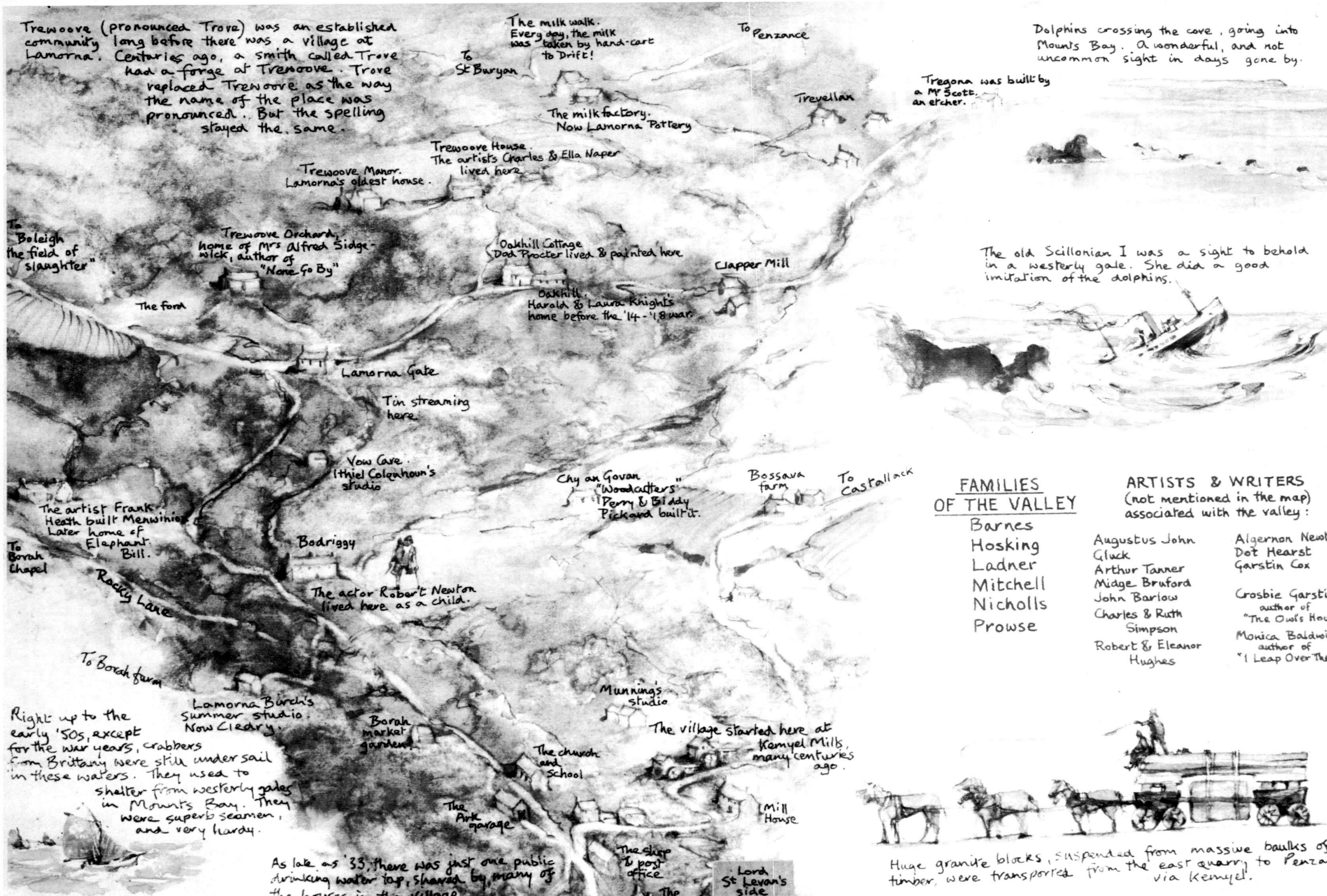
Trewoove (pronounced Trove) was an established community long before there was a village at Lamorna. Centuries ago, a smith called Trove had a forge at Trewoove. Trove replaced Trewoove as the way the name of the place was pronounced. But the spelling stayed the same.
The milk walk. Every day, the milk was taken by hand-cart to Drift!
To St Buryan
To Penzance
The milk factory. Now Lamorna Pottery
Trevellan
Tregona was built by a Mr Scott, an etcher.
Dolphins crossing the cove, going into Mounts Bay. A wonderful, and not uncommon sight in days gone by.
Trewoove House. The artists Charles & Ella Naper lived here
Trewoove Manor. Lamorna's oldest house.
To Boleigh the field of slaughter"
Trewoove Orchard, home of Mrs Alfred Sidgewick, author of "None Go By"
Oakhill Cottage Dod Procter lived & painted here
Clapper Mill
Oakhill. Harold & Laura Knight's home before the '14-'18 war.
The old Scillonian I was a sight to behold in a westerly gale. She did a good imitation of the dolphins.
The ford
Lamorna Gate
Tin streaming here
Vow Cave. Ithiel Colquhoun's studio
Chy an Govan "Woodcutters" Perry & Biddy Pickard built it.
Bossava farm
To Castallack
The artist Frank Heath built Menwinion Later home of Elephant Bill.
To Borah Chapel
Rocky Lane
Bodriggy
The actor Robert Newton lived here as a child.
FAMILIES OF THE VALLEY
Barnes
Hosking
Ladner
Mitchell
Nicholls
Prowse
ARTISTS & WRITERS (not mentioned in the map) associated with the valley:
Augustus John
Gluck
Arthur Tanner
Midge Bruford
John Barlow
Charles & Ruth Simpson
Robert & Eleanor Hughes
Algernon Newton
Dot Hearst
Garstin Cox
Crosbie Garstin author of "The Owl's House"
Monica Baldwin author of "I Leap Over The W
To Borah farm
Munnings' studio
Lamorna Birch's summer studio. Now Cleary.
Borah market garden.
The village started here at Kemyel Mills, many centuries ago.
Right up to the early '50s, except for the war years, crabbers from Brittany were still under sail in these waters. They used to shelter from westerly gales in Mounts Bay. They were superb seamen, and very hardy.
The church and school
The Ark garage
Mill House
The shop & post office
As late as '33, there was just one public drinking water tap, shared by many of the houses in the village.
Lord St Levan's side
Huge granite blocks, suspended from massive baulks of timber, were transported from the east quarry to Penzance via Kemyel.

Map of Lamorna Valley Yesterdays

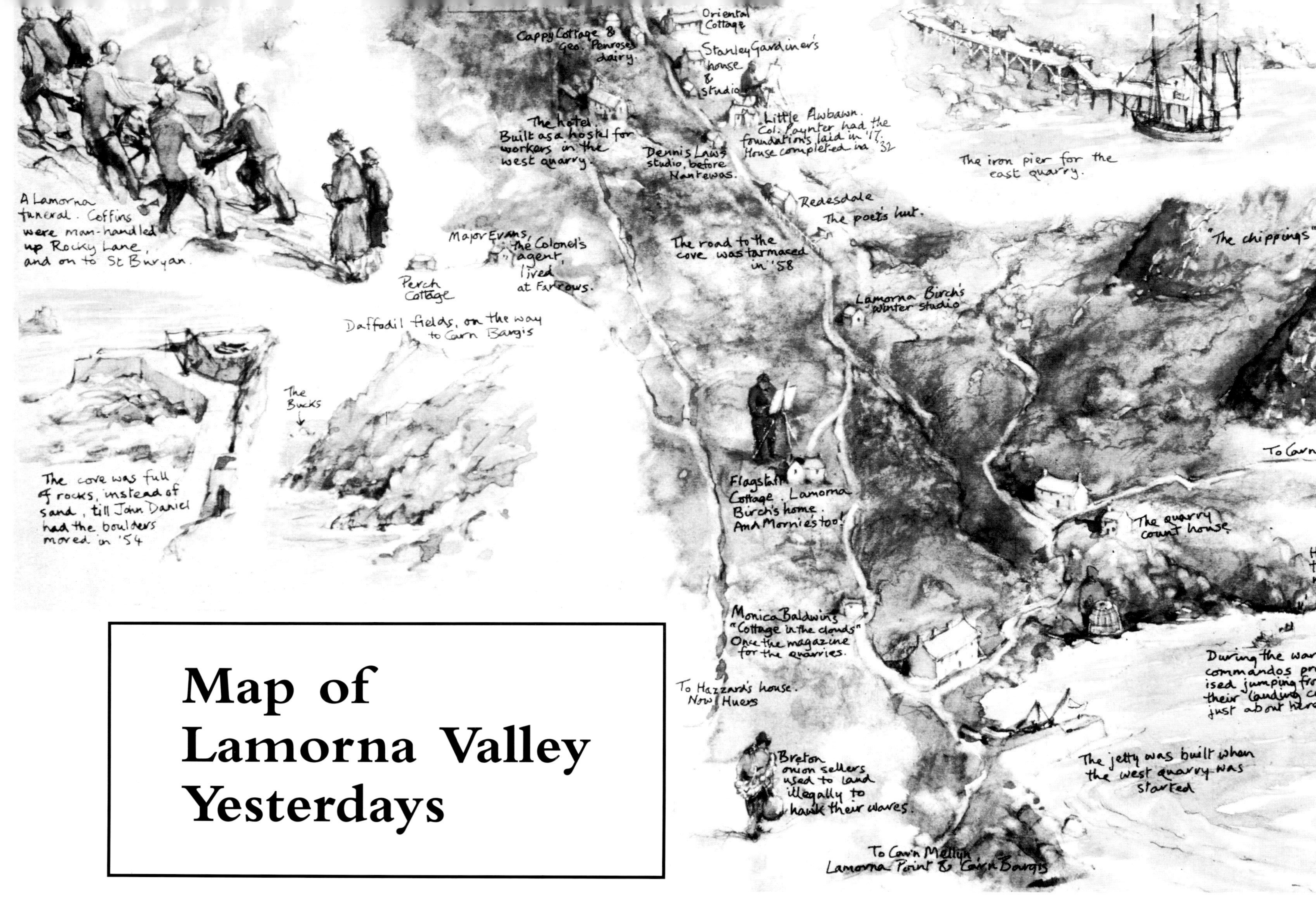

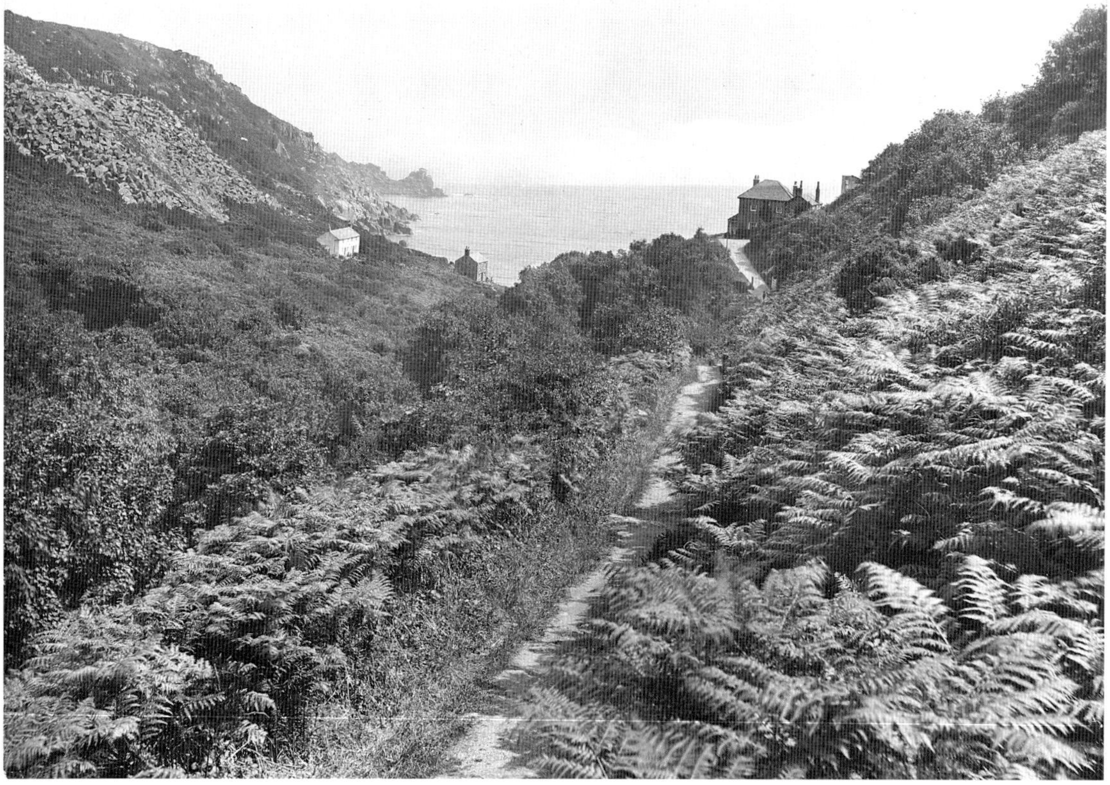

Lamorna Cove circa 1920.

The headland of Carn Du can be seen past the quarries on the left. The house, on the right, is Flagstaff Cottage, home of Lamorna Birch.

west along the cliff path one comes upon an improbable cross erected in memory of a student from Jesus College, Cambridge who fell to his death in 1873. Continuing further, following the zig-zag path, one soon arrives at Carn Barges, a mass of granite standing upright on the top of the cliff like a gigantic chair.

Plates 14 and 15 show two aspects of Carn Barges - by day and by night. The point where Frank Heath set up his easel was approached from Dorminack Farm (now the house of the author, Derek Tangye); this farm was at that time a 40 acre small holding occupied by Harry Ladner and his wife Elizabeth. Harry was the son of Joe (who lived at Perch Cottage, Lamorna and featured in Harold Knight's painting on Page 23). Frank Heath used to walk the two miles from Menwinnion to Dorminack carrying his easel, paintbox and large canvases. As the works progressed, Harry Ladner allowed him to store the canvases at the farm.

Much of the history of Lamorna is connected with the quarries. The largest and most notable was on the east side of the cove where the mined granite was of high quality. In the 19th century, hundreds of tons of stone were removed for building purposes, perhaps the biggest project being that of the Embankment in London. Standing below the face of the quarries with huge rocks strewn around, each cubic yard weighing approximately three tons, it is not difficult to imagine what great skill and exertion were necessary to

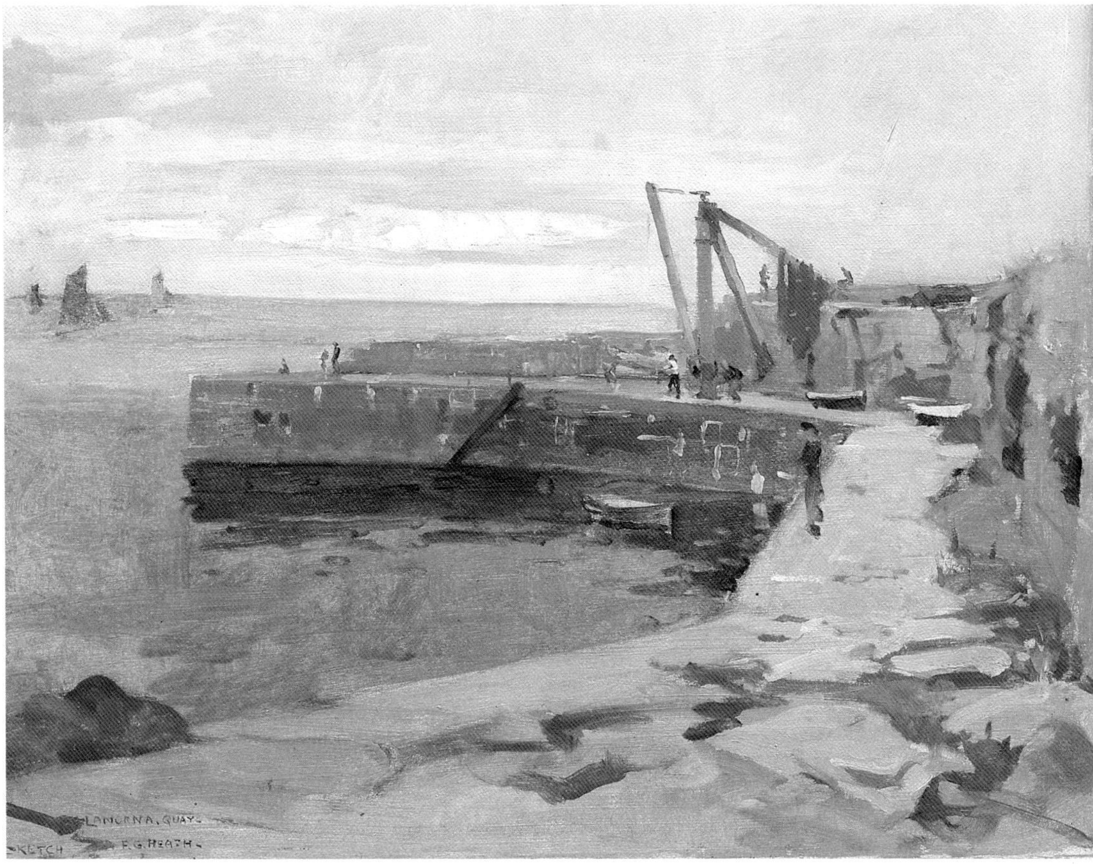

Lamorna Cove by Frank Heath   Oil 20" x 24"

This painting shows the quay and derrick at the cove. The jib was removed during the 2nd World War by the US Army to ensure that it would be of no assistance to the Germans following a possible landing.

blast the massive chunks from the face, chip away the spurious parts and load the huge blocks onto the sturdy, horse drawn, wagons ready for the hazardous journey via Kemyel and Newlyn to Wherry Town, near Penzance where the stone was cut up before being loaded into ships. The journey must have been hard and dangerous; the weights were enormous and the roads rough and primitive. In rain, thick mud clogged the iron clad wheels while dry weather encouraged choking dust to mark the progress of the struggling team. Perhaps the most formidable obstacle was Paul Hill, the steep hill down into Newlyn. With drag chains fitted and horses reined tight, the wagons slithered and bumped downwards and great skill must have been required to bring the team safely to the bottom.

A quarry was also developed on the west side of the cove. Rather than undertake the arduous journey overland, a quay and derrick were constructed in order to ship the granite direct to Penzance. This quarry was never a success due to the predominance of quartz in the rock and was soon closed down.

The centre of village life was the Lamorna Inn, also known as "The Wink". This name originated from the Inn's beginning as a temperance house when the only way to get a drink of spirits was to tip the landlord "the wink".

Robert Matthews ran the village shop which was next door to "The Wink". His

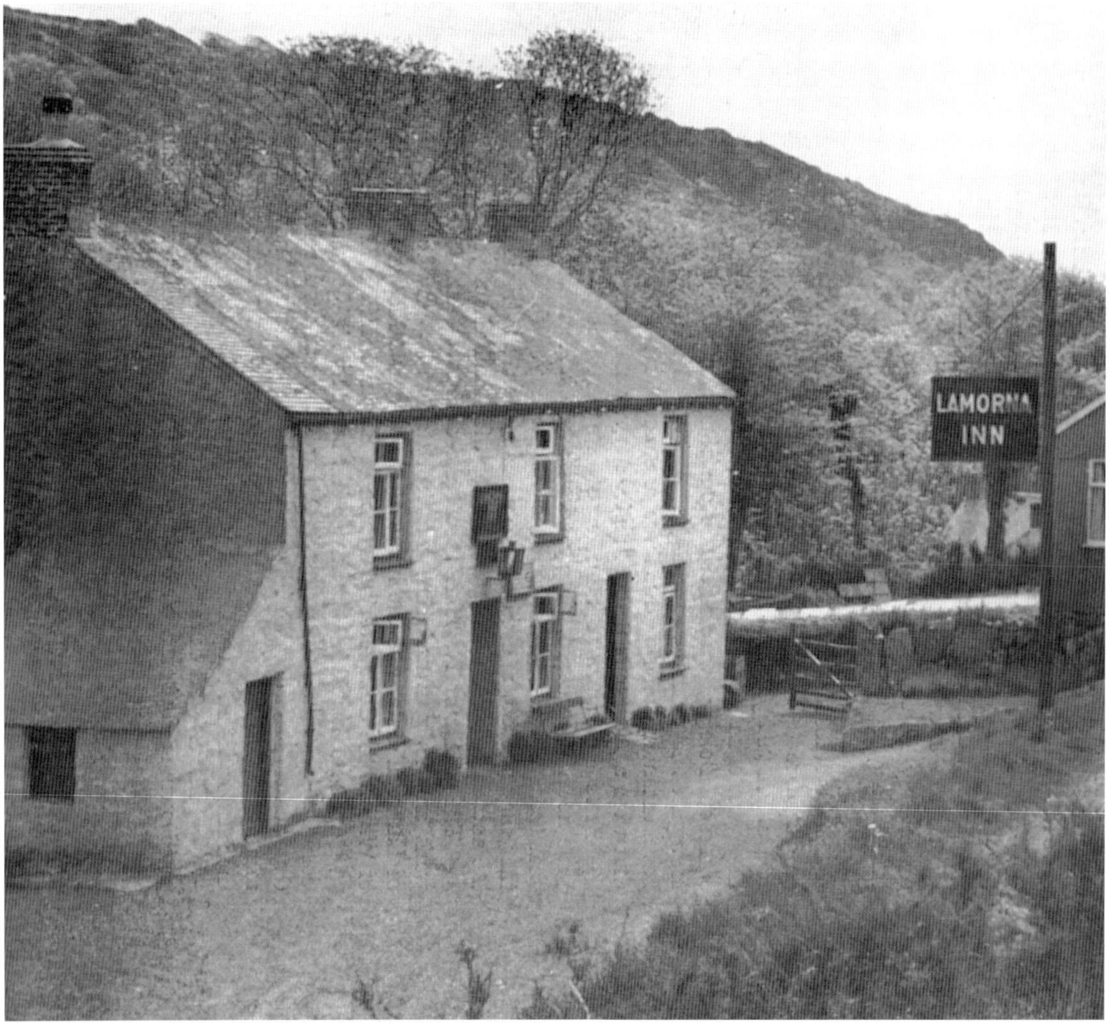

Lamorna Inn, also known as "The Wink"

nickname was "Locky" which sounds most appropriate as he had a reputation of being very tight. When he weighed anything he would bend level with the scales on the counter to make sure he would not give overweight. He was known to take a sweet from a bag he was weighing, bite half off it, eat it and return the other half to the bag.

Nick Jory (commonly known as "Old Jory") was a great character. His wife, to whom he never spoke, ran a "temperance establishment" at Cliff House (now the Lamorna Cove Hotel) about 100 yards distant. "Old Jory" enjoyed his drink. He had a pony called Albert and on one occasion left a party at a friend's house very much the worse for wear and fell asleep in the cart. He woke up back at "The Wink", Albert having found his own way home.

The present day Inn has its walls and ceiling covered in memorabilia of the sea including pictures and souvenirs of the dramatic attempted rescue of "The Flying Enterprise" off the South Cornwall coast in the early 1950s.

Cliff House was built in 1850 as the Quarry Manager's house and as a hostel for the quarry workers; within the building was a baptist chapel and a reminder of that early purpose is the bell tower still to be seen. (See page 24.)

When run by Mrs Jory, in the early part of the century, it was a lively place with parties

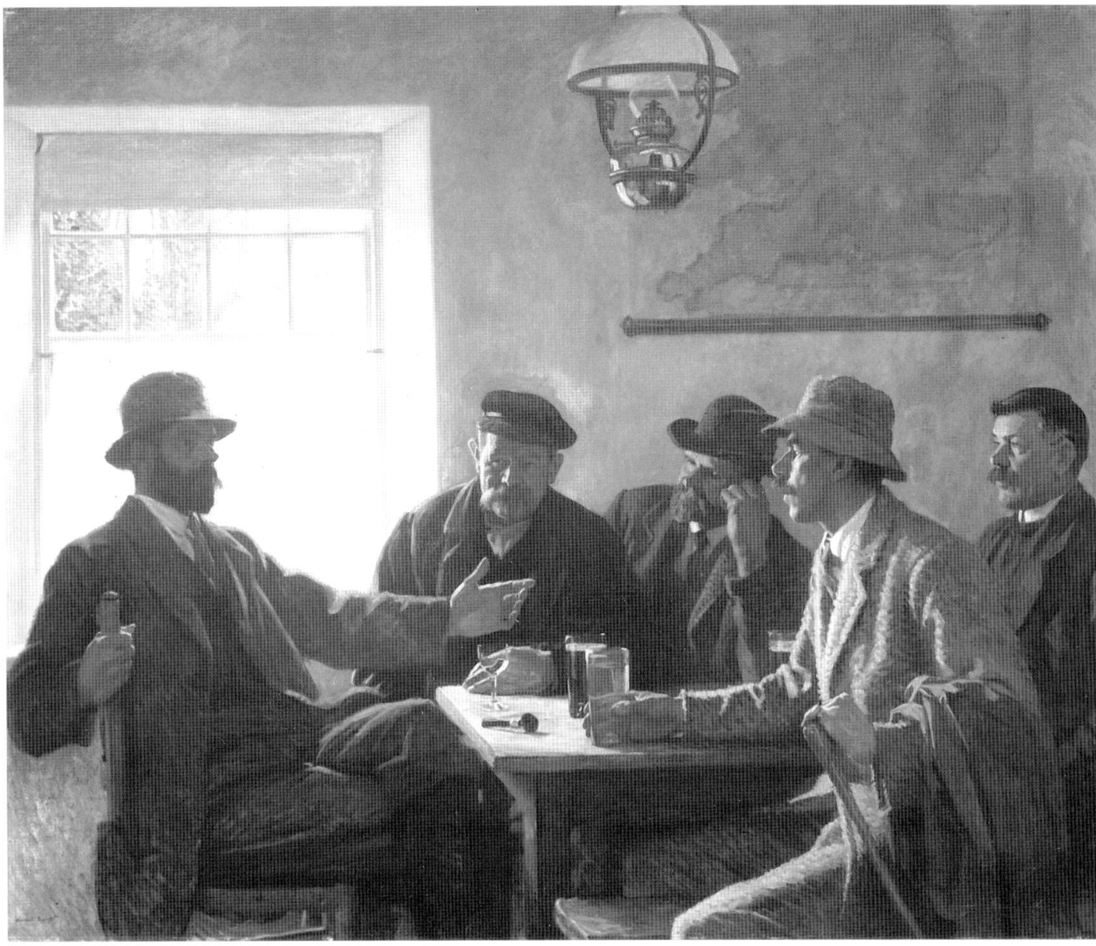

"The Council" by Harold Knight

This picture, painted by Harold Knight in 1916, shows some of the "regulars" enjoying a lunchtime drink at the Lamorna Inn. On the left is Lamorna Birch looking towards the figure of Robert Hughes (both artists living at Lamorna.) The other three figures are, from the left, Joe Ladner (one of the members of a family long established in the valley), Robert Matthews and Nick Jory, the landlord of the Inn.

and dances. After their marriage in 1912, Alfred Munnings and his wife, Florence lived at Cliff House and the invitation to a New Year's eve party, shown on page 27, was issued by them to Frank and Jessica Heath.

In 1913 Augustus John and his wife, Dorelia stayed at Cliff House for a few months. Laura Knight described her impressions on meeting them ".... John was powerful and broad-shouldered, his beard was tawny, his hair long, and he wore a tweed suit that had a thread of colour in it running both ways into a check; his shoes were cut dead square at the toes, had long vamps and wide laces. Mrs John wore the same kind of footwear. Her looks were startling in their rarity; it was easy to see the inspiration she might be to a painter. Her skin was ivory, her hair black; as she sat that evening with her hands folded like the "Mona Lisa" portrait, her long, tapering, white fingers and beautifully kept nails impressed me profoundly. It was impossible to take your eyes off her for long. Her clothes were of her own style, and it was she who set the fashion for jumpers and short hair; out-of-doors she wore a long black cape. We had parties and dances at Mrs Jory's. When feats of strength were being tried, we were amazed at John's athleticism - he was quite an acrobat."

One can imagine the villagers' reactions at the Johns' bohemian appearance and lifestyle. It was so very different from that of their own artists who were always smartly dressed. One of the inhabitants said it was shocking to see Mrs John walking in the lane without a hat, and "On Sunday too!"

While at Lamorna, Augustus produced some fine studies of Dorelia out on the rocks. He was delighted with his stay and later wrote "There are some extraordinary nice people there among the artists and some very attractive young girls among the people." One of these was Nancy Heath who was scared stiff that she would be kissed by him out on the rocks.

Fishing also played its part in the life of the village. The picture,"The Store Pot" (Plate 26) shows Ben Jeffery and Mr Whiting, the main fishermen of the cove in the 1920s. Ben lived later in Mousehole and became coxwain of the Penlee lifeboat.

On the road at the top of the valley lies Boleigh. Boleigh means "the field of slaughter" as it was near to here, in 936 AD, that Athelston defeated the Cornish. The picture in Plate 12, painted by Frank Heath in the early 1920s, shows a cart loaded with milk churns returning from the butter factory at Trevider. Every day, milk from all the farms roundabout was taken for separation at the butter factory and on the way back drivers would stop at Clapper Mill (see page 42) to have a sack of corn ground. On arrival back at the farm, the separated milk and corn husks were then mixed together as pig swill. In the mornings, milk carts were numerous on the local roads. The cart in the picture has

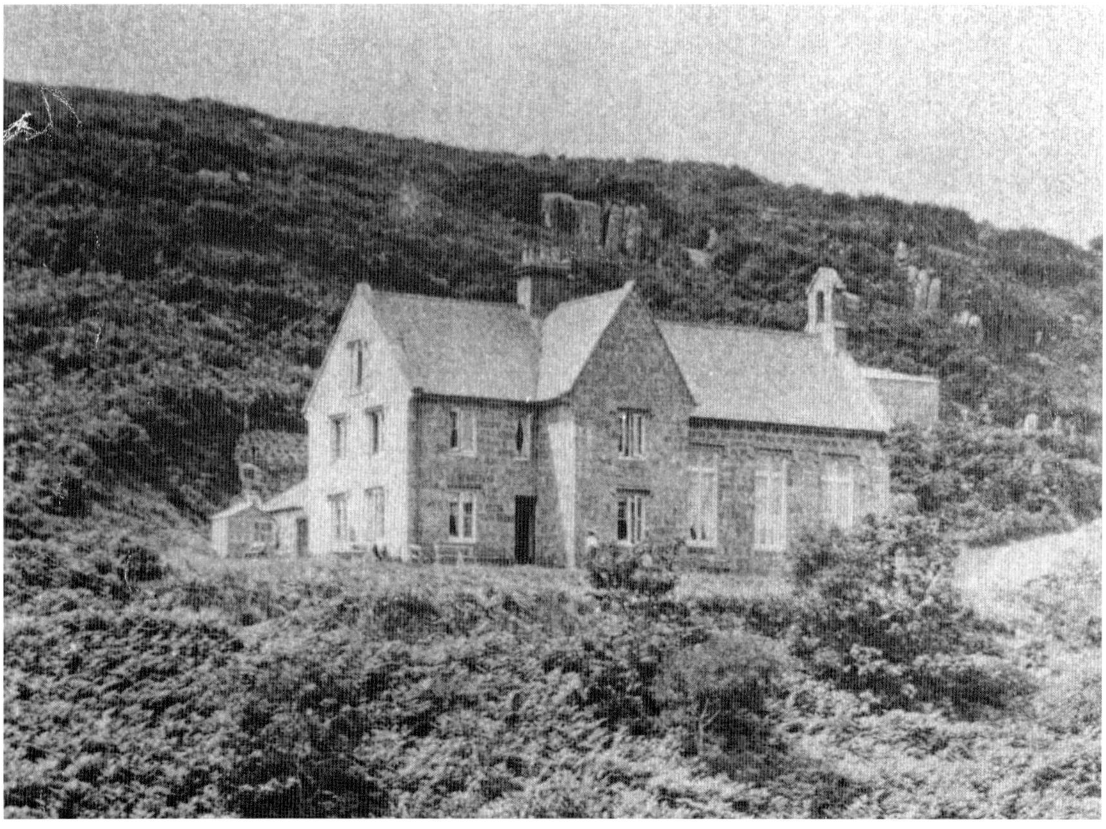

Cliff House, Lamorna (circa 1900)

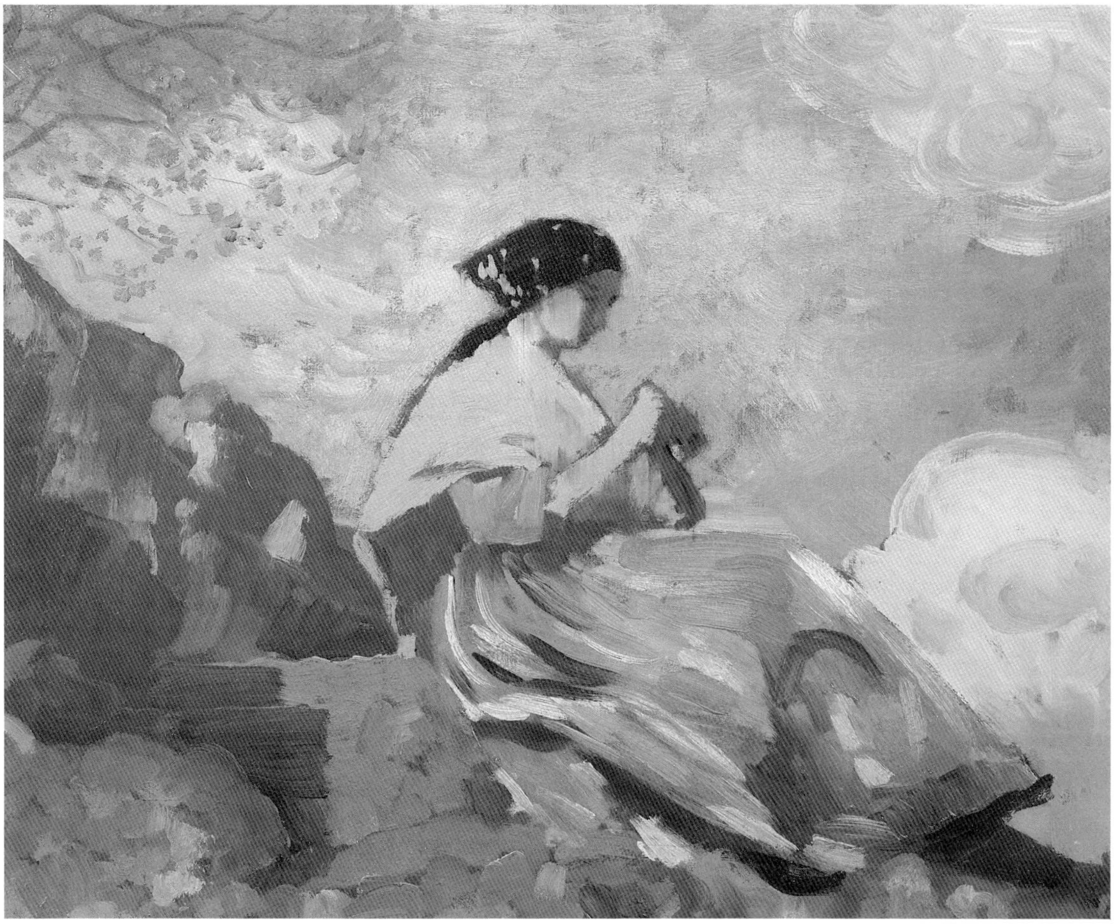

Dorelia by Augustus John

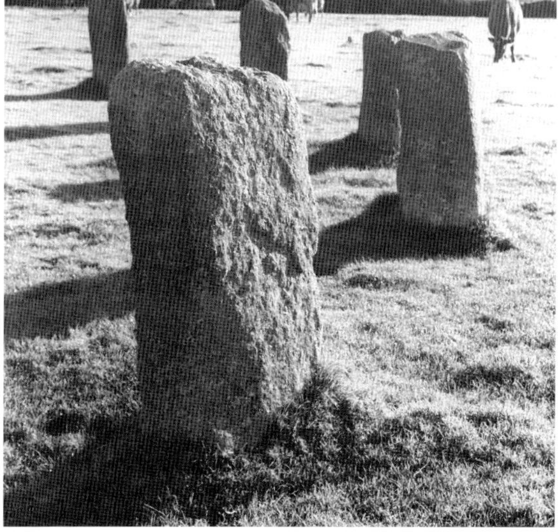

Five of "The Merry Maidens"

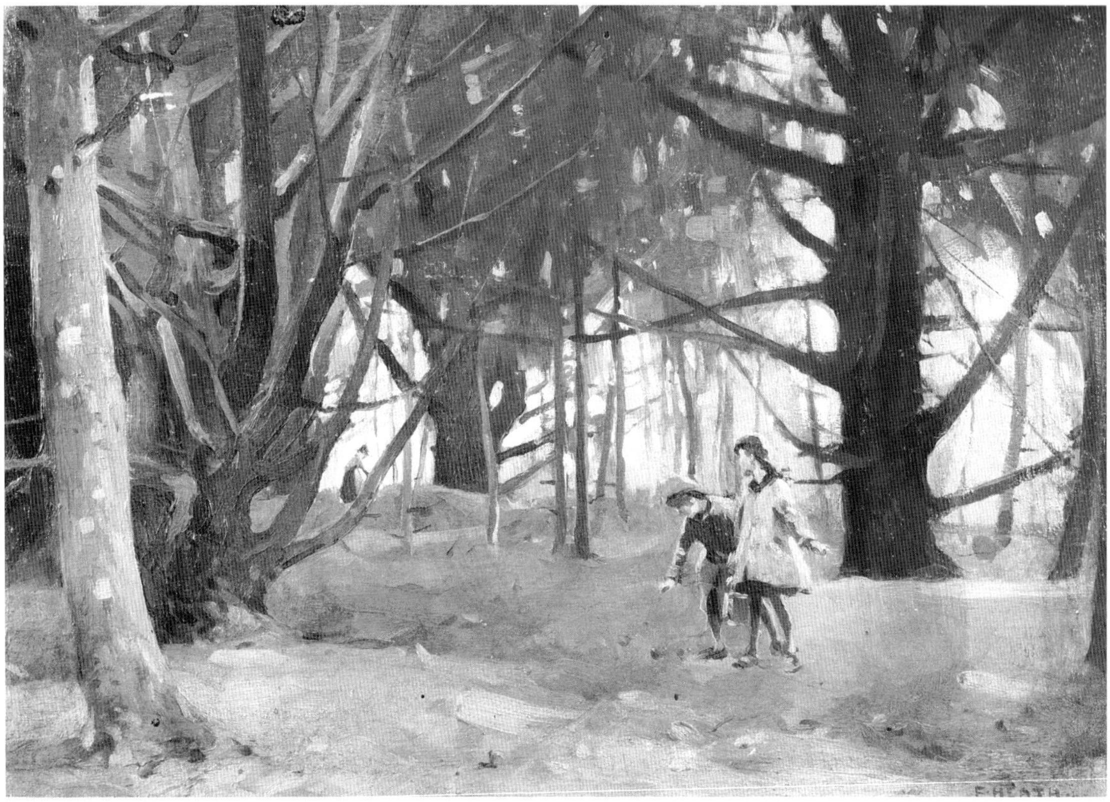

"The Witch" by Frank Heath Oil 10" x 14"

just reached the less steep section of Boleigh Hill (the road continues on to St Buryan) and is approaching Boleigh Farm.

The sources of many legends and interesting relics are to be found throughout Cornwall and some of these are in the Lamorna area. Just beyond Boleigh Farm can be seen in a field, "the Pipers of Boleigh", two large gaunt stone pillars, twelve feet high. In another field nearby is a circle of nineteen stones, known as "The Merry Maidens". Legend has it that the maidens were dancing and making merry to the music of the pipers on the Sabbath and were consequently all turned to stone. These stones are the most famous Cornish circle.

Also travelling by road from Lamorna towards Newlyn is Trevelloe Wood with its stories of black magic and witchcraft. "The Witch", above, depicts Aileen and Nancy, Frank Heath's eldest two children walking in Trevelloe Wood. An alternative title for the picture being "....Hello little redcap!" - a comment shouted at the girls by a passing farmer. The two startled girls, thinking that they were trespassing ran home to their father who then painted the scene - replacing the farmer with a witch. (Certainly, the woods had a reputation locally for strange rituals.)

Why did so many of the second generation of Newlyn artists make their home in and around Lamorna in the early part of this century? It could have been its outstanding natural beauty (with its proximity to the sea and neighbouring countryside) and its peace and tranquility (with so few cars, visitors were rare), that made it a more attractive proposition than Newlyn. It was into this atmosphere and environment that Frank and Jessica Heath arrived in 1912, to organize the building of Menwinnion which was to become their family home for over 20 years.

An invitation to a New Year's Eve party issued by Alfred and Florence Munnings to Frank and Jessica Heath in 1912.

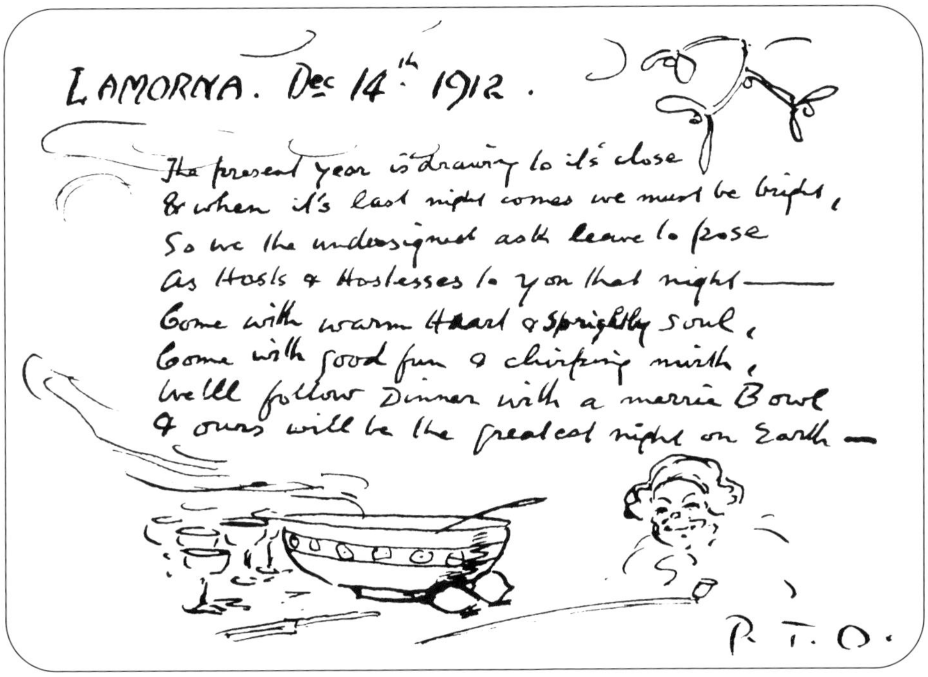

LAMORNA. Dec 14th 1912.

The present year is drawing to it's close
& when it's last night comes we must be bright,
So we the undersigned ask leave to pose
As Hosts & Hostesses to you that night —
Come with warm Heart & Sprightly Soul,
Come with good fun & chirping mirth,
We'll follow Dinner with a merrie Bowl
& ours will be the greatest night on Earth —

R.T.O.

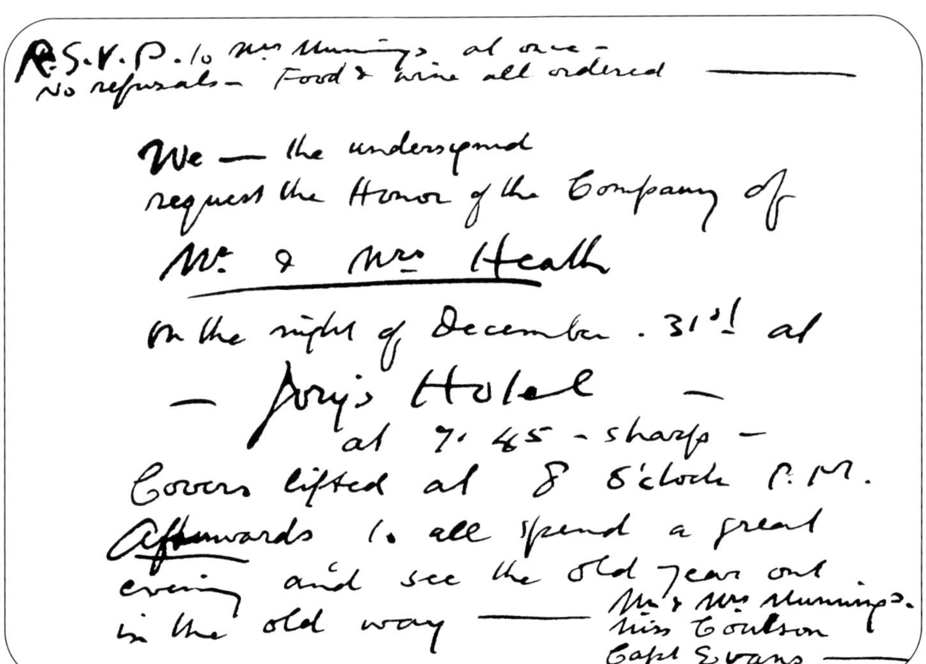

R.S.V.P. to Mrs Munnings at once —
No refusals — Food & wine all ordered —

We — the undersigned
request the Honor of the Company of
Mr & Mrs Heath
on the night of December. 31st at
— Jory's Hotel —
at 7.45 - sharp -
Covers lifted at 8 o'clock P.M.
Afterwards to all spend a great
evening and see the Old Year out
in the old way —

Mr & Mrs Munnings.
Miss Coulson
Capt Evans —

Chapter 3

MENWINNION AND THE WAR YEARS

After their two years at Polperro, Frank and Jessica Heath decided to move back to the Newlyn area and settle at Lamorna where Jessica's father paid for the building of a family house for them as a belated wedding present.

One of the large landowners around Lamorna at that time was Colonel Paynter who lived at Boskenna and it was from him that Frank Heath purchased 10 acres of land at the top of the valley on which to build a house. The architect was Mr Stacey who lived locally and the house was built by the Matthews family from Newshop, St Buryan. The land, when bought, was just a scrubland field enclosed by a stone wall. As was then common, granite from which the house was built, was hand drilled out of the ground on the site and then split and shaped into the sizes of blocks required.

The house took a year to build, cost £1000 and was christened Menwinnion meaning "House of the Winds". It consisted, on the ground floor, of a hall, morning and dining rooms, kitchen, scullery and cloakroom; upstairs were 5 bedrooms, a bathroom and two attic rooms. Frank and Jessica with their two young children moved into their new home in 1913.

The design and landscaping of the large garden were both major challenges. Within

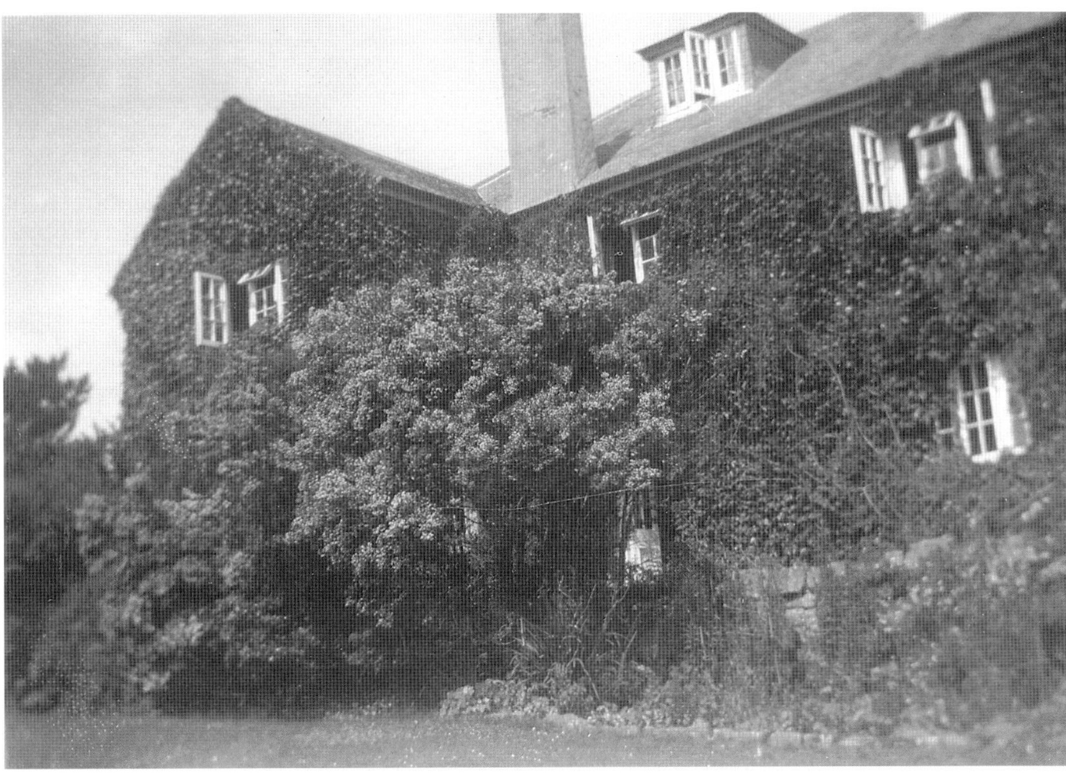

Menwinnion (circa 1930)

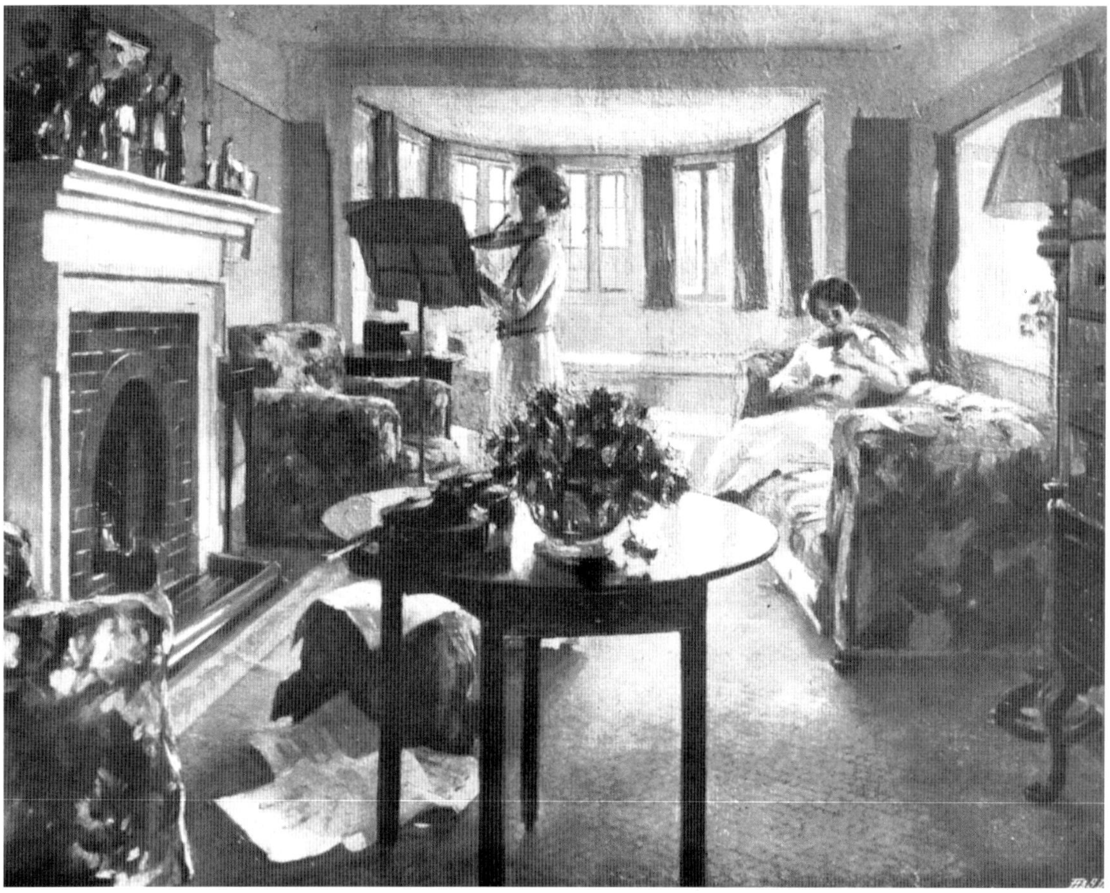

The Morning Room at Menwinnion by Frank Heath. (Jessica is playing the violin.)
Exhibited at the Royal Academy 1914.

the garden, Cornish stone walls were constructed and privet and escallonia hedges planted as windbreaks. From the holes made by the excavation of the granite, several 'courts' were created and named - "Lavender", "May" and "Wood"; below these courts a pond was also dug out. The bottom half of the garden was planted with quick growing pine and it was here that Frank Heath built his first studio. He subsequently built another adjoining the main house. (Laura Knight's studio, also built on wild land provided by Colonel Paynter, was situated at the bottom of the Heath's garden.)

During the building of Menwinnion, the family lived nearby at The Red House (by Trevelloe Wood).

The War Years

Early in the War, Frank Heath, along with other Lamorna artists, Benje Leader and Joey Carter-Wood, volunteered for active service. Robert Hughes was adjudged medically unfit while Lamorna Birch and Harold Knight took up work on the land. Frank enlisted in Lady Cunliffe Lister's 2nd Sportsmans Battalion of the Artists Rifles (Royal Fusiliers). After undergoing basic training at Romford, he was posted to France in the Spring of 1915. Soon after his arrival at the front he suffered badly from the effects of the German chlorine gas attacks and was admitted to hospital. His condition deteriorated and

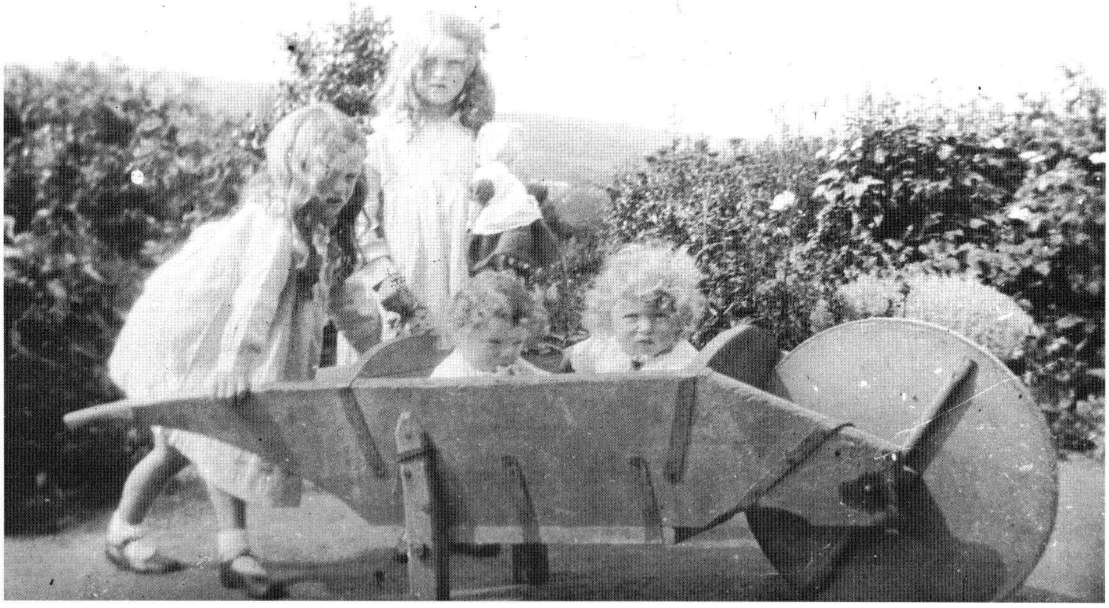

The Wheelbarrow. From the left, Nancy, Aileen, Gabriel and Tony

such was Jessica's anxiety that she and a doctor travelled to France where she insisted on his return to England for treatment. She arranged for him to be brought back and he was admitted to hospital in London where he was diagnosed as having cerebral meningitis. The severity of the illness led him to being invalided out of the army and returned to Menwinnion to convalesce.

After his return, Frank continued with his painting. However, from the outbreak of the war, severe restrictions against painting any part of the coastline came into force under the Defence of the Realm Regulations. These regulations were strongly enforced and artists were forbidden to work out of doors at all. Local people were recruited for patrolling and coastwatching; they had the powers of stop and search, of arrest without warrant and to use force, if resistance was encountered. Any painting or sketch could be confiscated and if more serious, a fine or imprisonment could follow.

An artist in a letter to the Times in 1915 wrote ".... may I complain of the very drastic rules against artists or anyone sketching about the coast of Cornwall. It seems to me at a time like this, when painters are hard put to find any sale for their work, the authorities might give permits to artists or others to go on with their work around the coast - provided, of course, they were people who could be absolutely trusted. .... I was spotted one Sunday afternoon; my sketchbook was taken away by the coastwatcher who said that it would probably be destroyed." It was not until 1917 that the restrictions were eased and artists could apply for permits for painting out of doors.

The war years cannot have been easy for Jessica at Menwinnion. Aileen and Nancy were still under school age and the twins, Tony and Gabriel were born in 1915. She also had to help Frank recover following his illness. Food was short; vegetables and fruit were grown in the garden and eggs, butter and pork were available from the surrounding farms.

At Menwinnion. From the left, Aileen, Tony, Gabriel and Nancy.

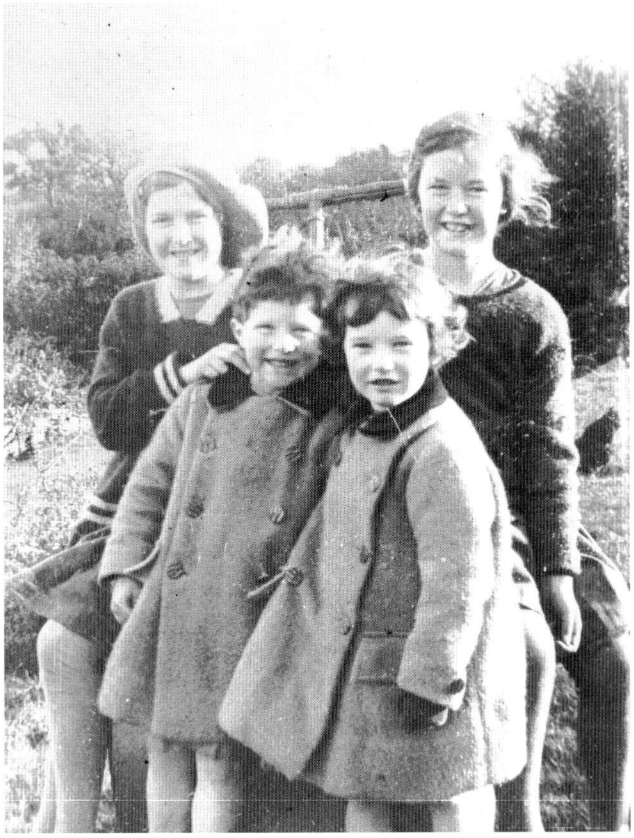

Jessica's parents were now living at "Polwithen Lodge" in Penzance and sent out groceries by carrier.

During the war, Aileen and Nancy spent periods of time with their grandparents in Penzance. While there, Aileen received some delightful letters from her father (see pages 34 and 35). The first is written from Romford in March 1915 while he was undertaking his initial army training and before being taken ill. The other was written after his return to Menwinnion to recover.

Initially it was easy to obtain domestic help at Menwinnion and two maids were employed in the house; they were resident and had rooms in the attic. After the war only

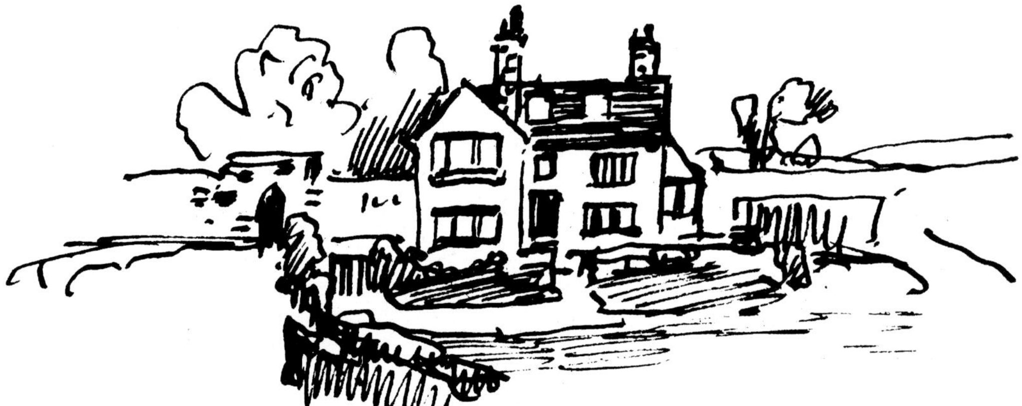

Sketch of Menwinnion by Frank Heath

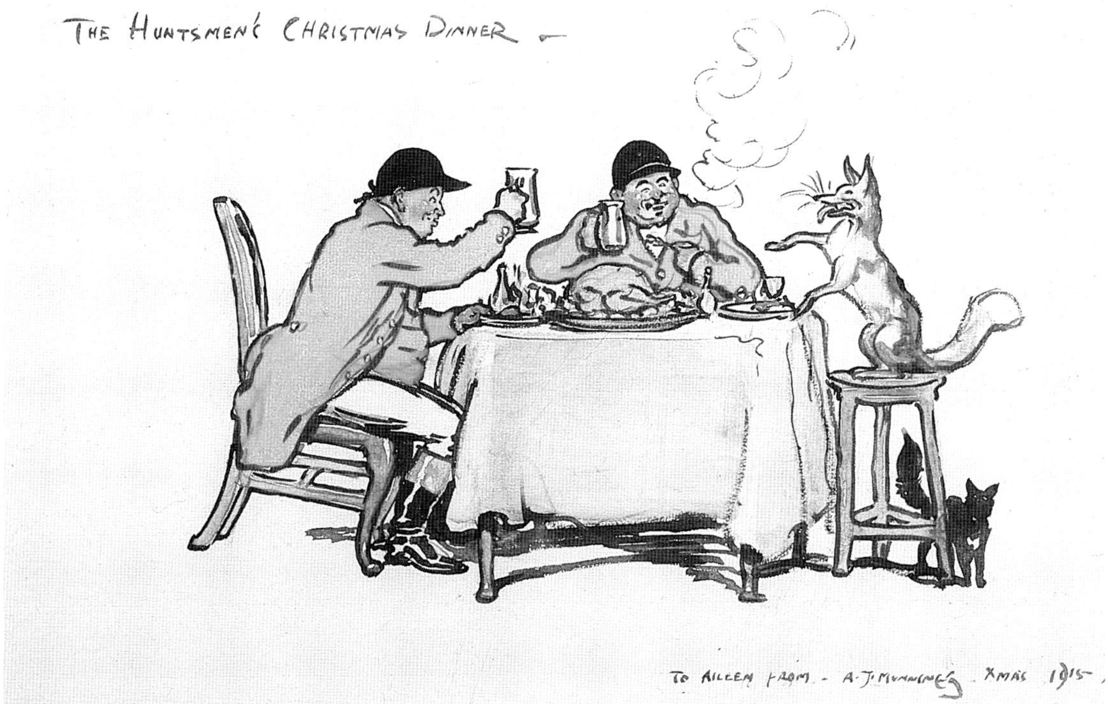

"The Huntsmen's Christmas Dinner" by A J Munnings

one local girl helped in the house. A gardener, Thomas, came in 3-4 days a week and was paid 5 shillings per day. Mrs Stick came up from the village to do all the washing by hand.

The water for the house had to be pumped up by hand from the well in the courts and this required one hour's pumping twice a week. In later years a mechanical pump was installed. The well also had another use. On hot summer days it was a good place to keep bottles of beer cool, ready for drinking.

Among the first visitors to Menwinnion were Alfred Munnings and his wife, Florence who became great friends of Jessica and Frank. In June 1914, Alfred Munnings wrote and illustrated the poem to Jessica shown on pages 36 to 38 . In it he recounts Jessica's feelings and thoughts during her evening horse ride. After the tragic death of Florence, Alfred Munnings stayed for periods of time with the Heaths at Menwinnion. While he was with them in the latter part of 1915 he painted the amusing "The Huntsmen's Christmas Dinner - To Aileen from A J Munnings Xmas 1915" (see above); Aileen was then five. At the same time, Munnings painted tiny pictures to help decorate the doll's house constructed by Frank Heath for his children. (See page 76.) In later years he painted similar pictures for Queen Mary's dolls house at Windsor and perhaps he got his ideas for this while at Menwinnion.

Another painter to stay often with Frank and Jessica from the end of the war was R C ("Seal") Weatherby. Seal was badly affected by the war and in 1918/9 recuperated at Menwinnion. He was one of the racing family associated with the Jockey Club and a great horseman. Before the war he was a frequent visitor to Newlyn (where he painted at Trewarveneth) and after the war to Lamorna (where he took over Munnings's studio near the Mill.) After leaving Lamorna he owned riding stables at the Lizard to which Nancy and Gabriel were visitors in the 1930s.

Letter from Frank Heath to his eldest daughter, Aileen, while he was undertaking his Army training at Hare Hall, Romford in March 1915.

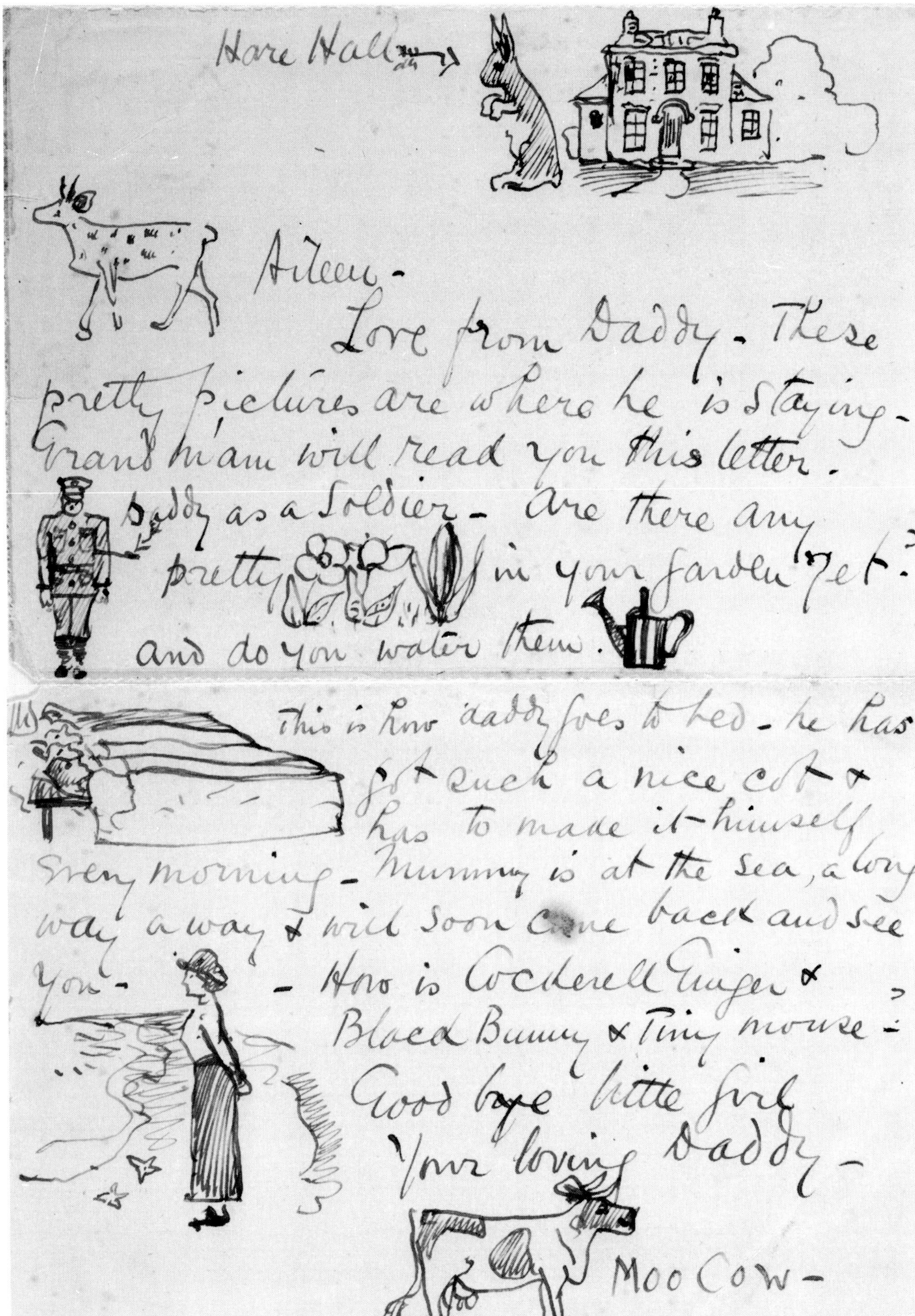
Hare Hall

Aileen -

Love from Daddy - These pretty pictures are where he is staying - Grand M'am will read you this letter. Daddy as a Soldier - Are there any pretty in your garden yet? and do you water them.

This is how daddy goes to bed - he has got such a nice cot & has to made it himself every morning - Mummy is at the sea, a long way away & will soon come back and see you - - How is Cockerell Ginger & Black Bunny & Tiny mouse? Good bye little girl Your loving Daddy -

MOO COW -

Letter from Frank Heath to Aileen when she was staying with her grandparents at Penzance in 1916.

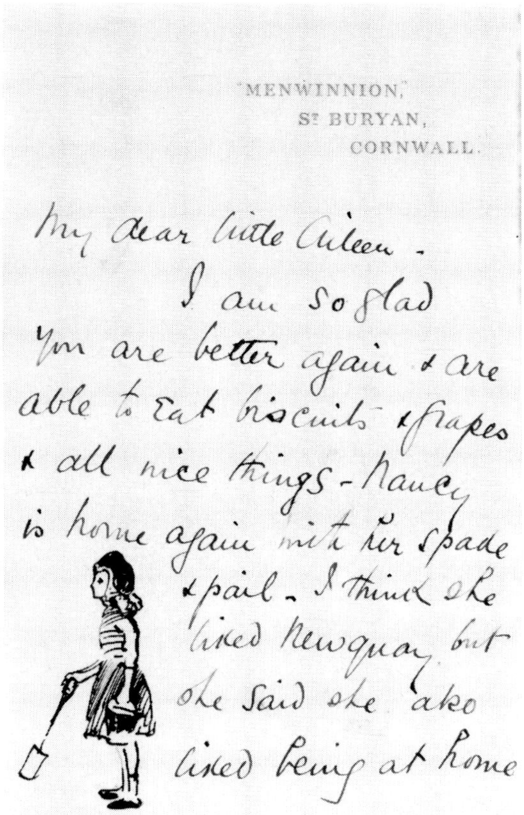

"MENWINNION,"
ST BURYAN,
CORNWALL.

My dear little Aileen -
I am so glad
you are better again & are
able to eat biscuits & grapes
& all nice things - Nancy
is home again with her spade
& pail - I think she
liked Newquay but
she said she also
liked being at home

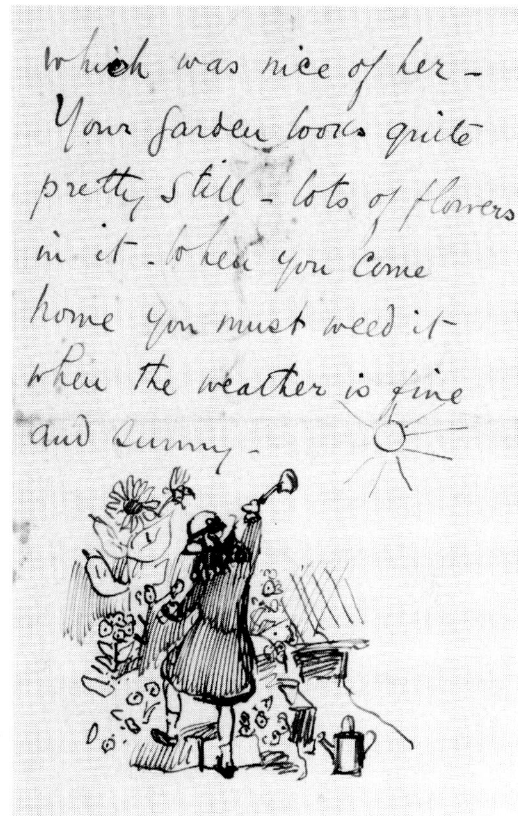

which was nice of her -
Your garden looks quite
pretty still - lots of flowers
in it - When you come
home you must weed it
when the weather is fine
and sunny -

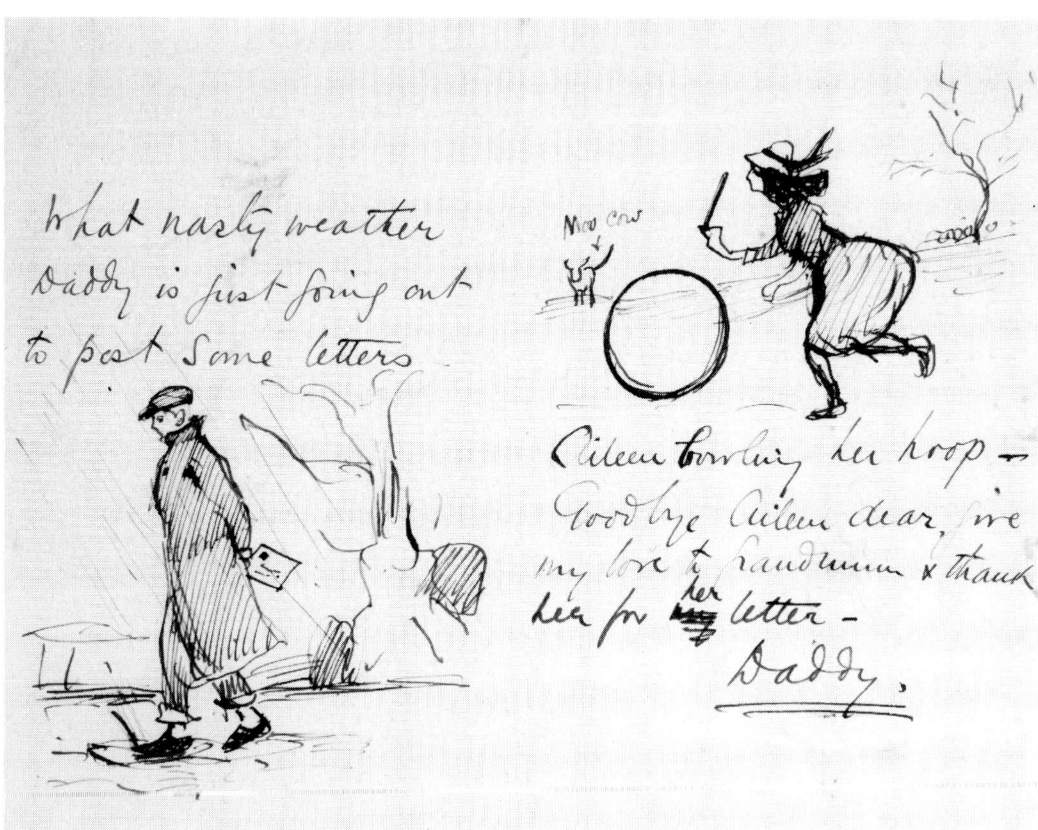

What nasty weather
Daddy is just going out
to post some letters

Moo cow

Aileen bowling her hoop -
Goodbye Aileen dear, give
my love to Grandmum & thank
her for her letter -
Daddy.

A poem to Jessica Heath written and illustrated by Alfred Munnings in June 1914.

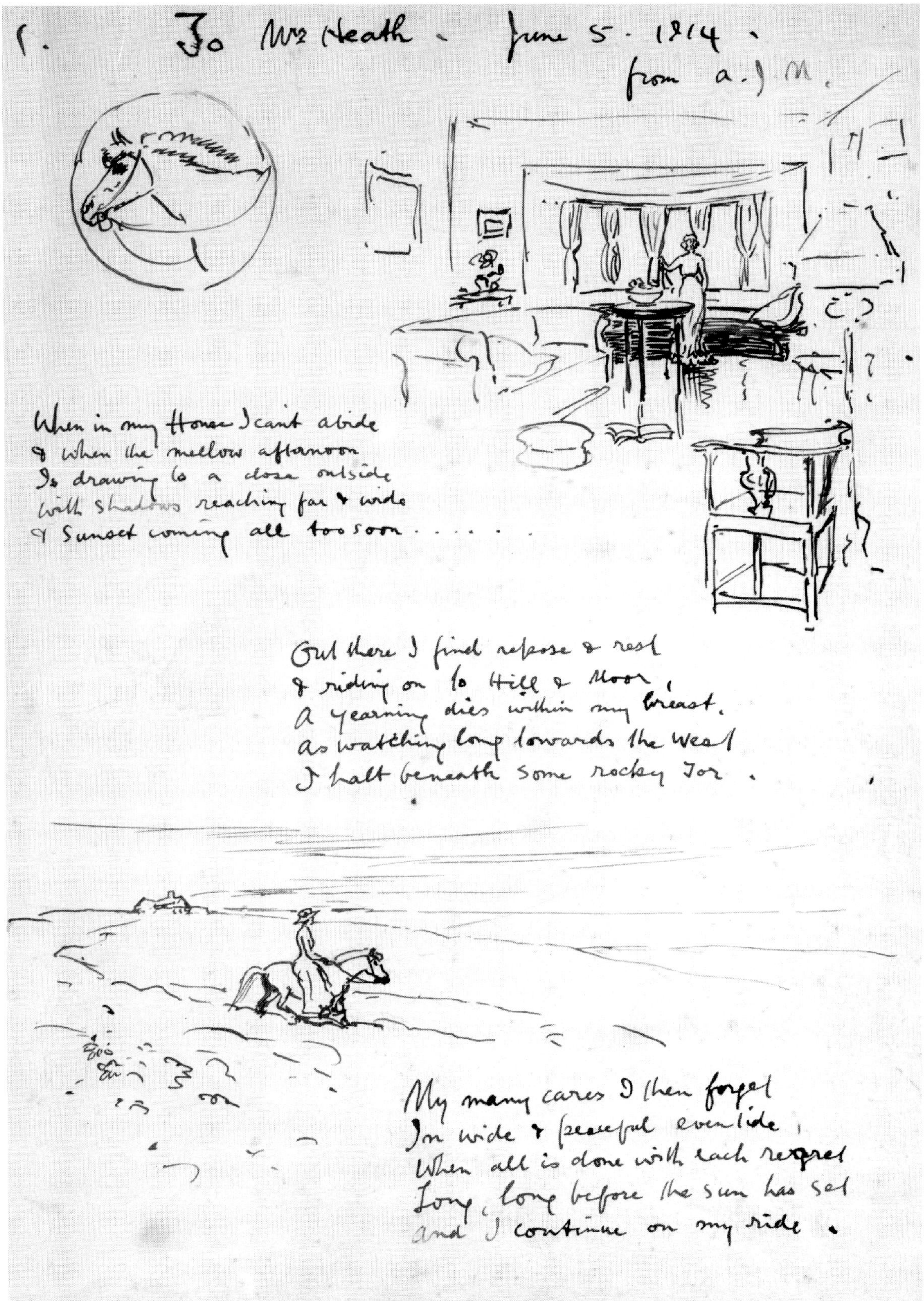

1. To Mrs Heath – June 5 · 1914 ·
from A. J. M.

When in my House I can't abide
& when the mellow afternoon
Is drawing to a close outside
With shadows reaching far & wide
& Sunset coming all too soon . . . . .

Out there I find repose & rest
& riding on to Hill & Moor,
A yearning dies within my breast.
As watching long towards the West
I halt beneath some rocky Tor .

My many cares I then forget
In wide & peaceful eventide,
When all is done with each regret
Long, long before the sun has set
And I continue on my ride .

2.

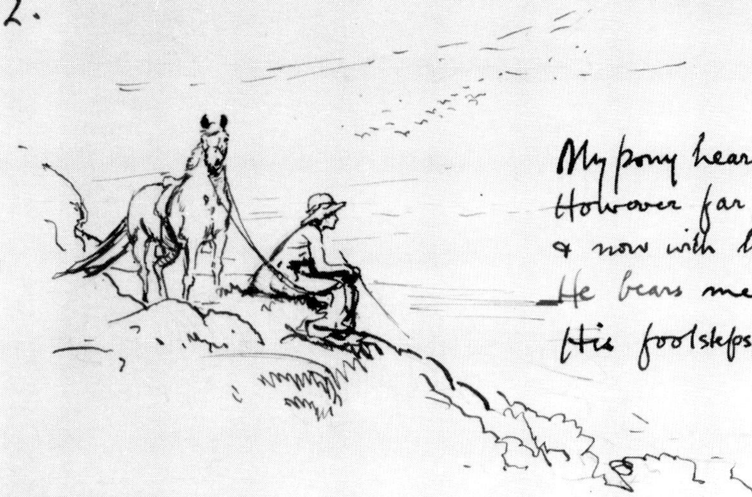

My pony hears each little sound.
However far, however near
& now with hurried step & bound
He bears me down a path new found
His footsteps sure, dispelling fear.

By footways tortuous & slow
We reach the cliffs & springy turf
Where granite rocks are piled below
& so like savage castles grow
arising from the sounding surf.

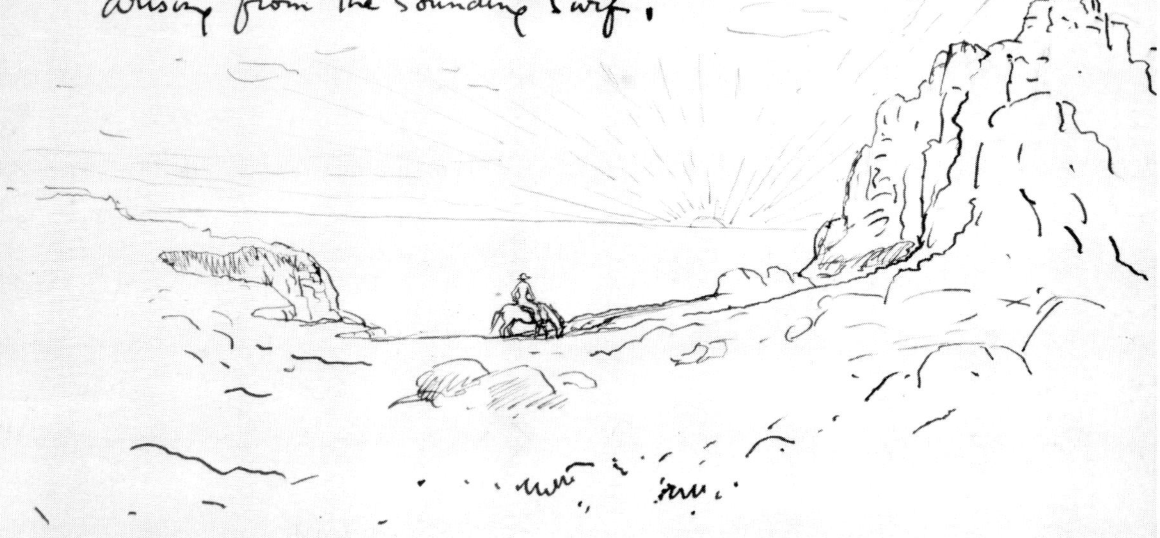

The sun has set, the air is still,
The west is gorgeous with it's gold,
A Blackbirds song with flute & trill
Echoing from a farther hill
Is with the sound of surf enrolled.

3.

The scent of gorse & heather sweet
The throbbing purple where the sea
& vast, long-stretching skyline meet
& drowsy surging 'neath my feet
Steal to the very Heart of me.

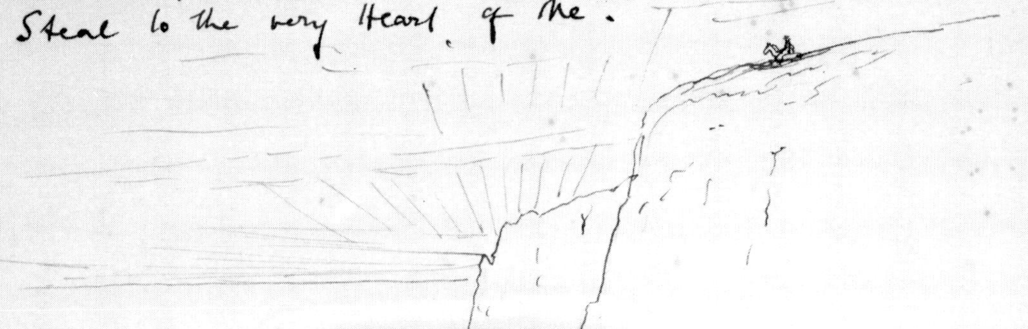

Before I leave, to all around
For one short space, I give my heart —
. . . .
All filled with color & with sound
The pulsing air — My heart spellbound
Is now both sad & loath to start —

. . . .

I break the spell — I ride away, —
& swiftly on my pony trots
Thro' twilit lanes of scented may
& home to where my babies lay
asleep within their little cots.

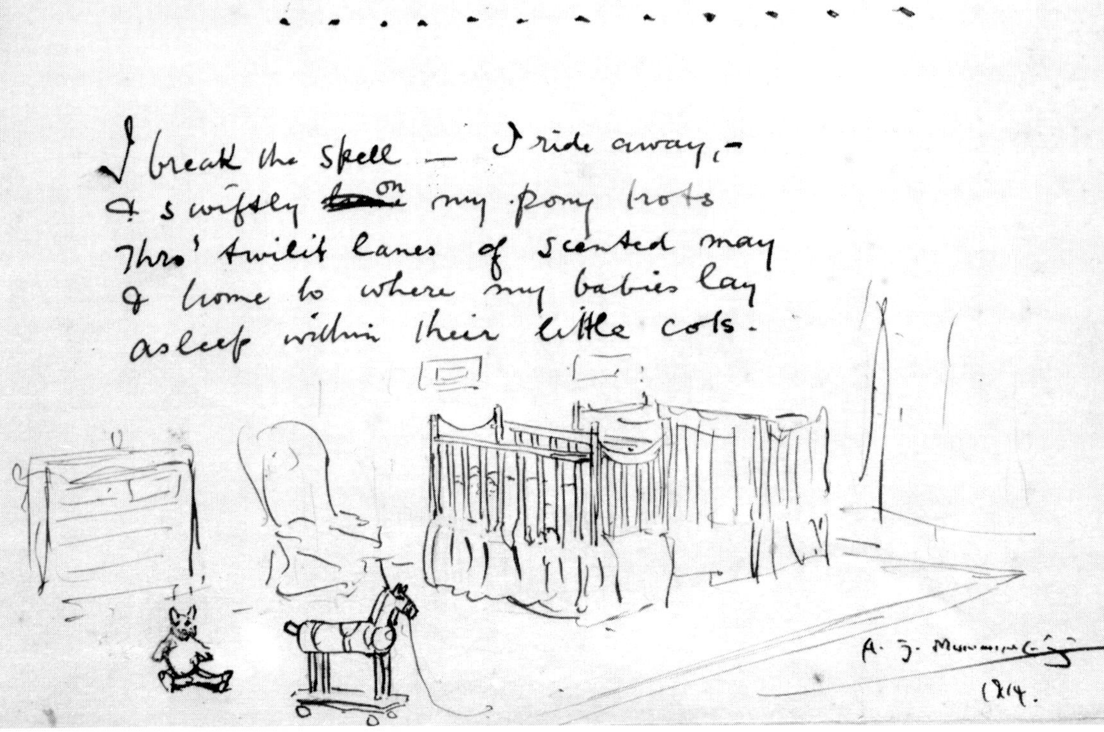

A. J. Munnings
1914.

Chapter 4

THE PAINTER AND HIS "PICTURES AT AN EXHIBITION"

Frank Heath loved Lamorna and the majority of his pictures were painted at and around Menwinnion or on the nearby rocks overlooking the sea. He followed very much in the tradition of Bastien-Lepage and Stanhope Forbes by painting out of doors in the "plein air" style, although many of his pictures were finished in his studio. When

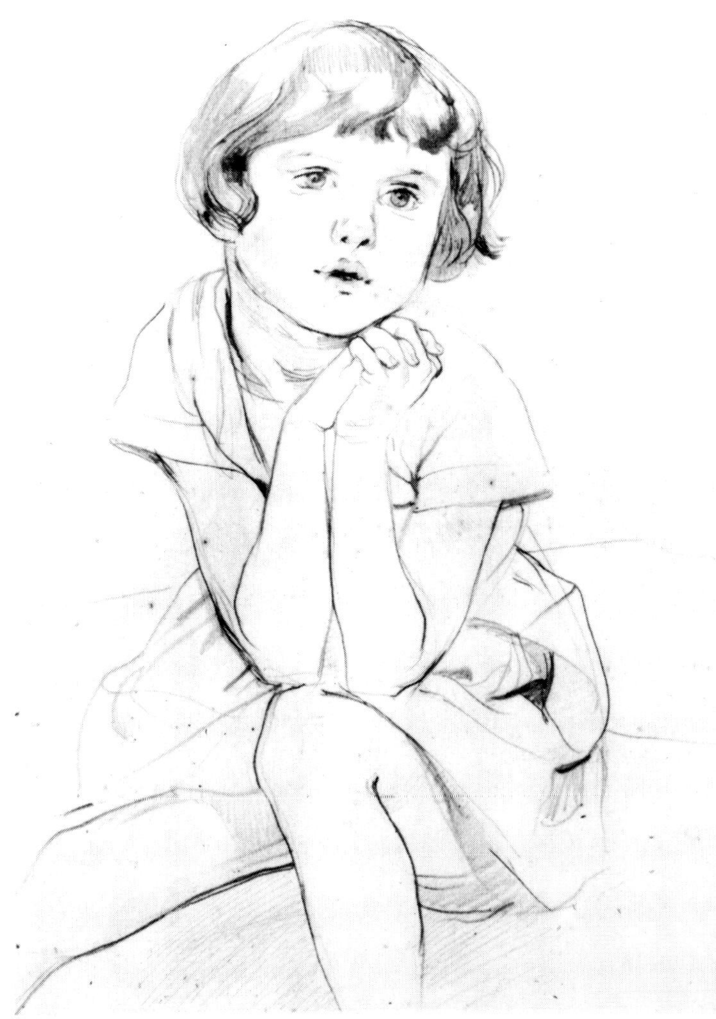

Gabriel by Frank Heath.
Pencil Sketch 11" x 9"

painting, he was always smartly dressed wearing a stiff collar, tweed coat, waistcoat and breeches. Each spring he would request samples of tweed to be sent to Menwinnion from his tailor in London and a new outfit was made for him annually.

Although his output was not prolific (unlike, for instance, Lamorna Birch and

Stanhope Forbes) he was very versatile in his range of subjects; he was equally at home whether painting animals, interiors, his garden, seascapes or his children.

A number of his pictures featured his children whom he used as models; they used to sit for many hours and were paid a few pence to supplement their pocket money. Also, if a picture of them was sold, he gave them a small share of the profits.

In his obituary in "The Times" of 23 June 1936, Frank Heath was described as "... having been for many years a popular member of the artistic colony at Newlyn, Cornwall and his most characteristic work was done in the Land's End district. Painting both the figure and landscape, he was essentially an open-air artist, direct in his methods with a good sense of values and a fine taste in colour." His use of colour was certainly a major feature in his work, as also was his fine technique in the use of light to enhance and bring out specific aspects of his compositions. "The Cornishman" in their reviews of the Newlyn Exhibitions of the 1920s refer to him as "the sunshine artist".

His style did not alter much over the years and he painted mainly in oils. The sizes of these pictures varied considerably from the large 5ft x 4ft canvases to some delightful small works produced on panels which fitted into the lid of his wooden paint box. He did, however, undertake small watercolour studies in preparation for larger works. For example,"Polperro" (Plate 9), painted in 1911 when living there soon after his marriage, was produced as a study for "Grey roofs beside a narrow wharf in cluster". This large oil was hung at the 1912 Liverpool Autumn Exhibition held at the Walker Art Gallery and was on offer for sale at £150.

In order to obtain the best positions from which to paint his pictures, Frank could be seen walking several miles from Menwinnion over fields, scrubland and rocks carrying his easel, paint box and canvas; the latter varied a great deal in size and transporting one, measuring 5ft x 4ft, cannot have been easy with the sea breezes and rough terrain.

All his paints and artist materials were purchased from Windsor and Newton in Chelsea. He made many of his own frames which showed a high degree of craftsmanship.

In the latter part of the 19th century, many of the "Newlyn School" paintings were destined for submission to the Royal Academy and as a preview to that annual exhibition, the artists opened their studios to the public for a few days in the Spring, before the works were sent to London. Many visitors came to Newlyn for this event and it is recorded that as many as 500 visitors would pass through a single studio during the "open" days. John Passmore Edwards, a Cornishman, who had spent much of his life in America building a considerable newspaper business and an equally considerable fortune, was one of these visitors. He was much impressed by the painters and their works and offered to build them a Gallery for the preview of the Academy paintings and other exhibitions. Permission for building was given and in 1895 the Gallery was opened, to be called the Passmore Edwards Art Gallery (now the Newlyn Art Gallery). In his time, Frank Heath was one of its best known exhibitors and many of his paintings were hung there before being sent up to London for submission to the Royal Academy.

There was always great excitement locally when news reached the artists on whether their pictures had been accepted by the Royal Academy for their Summer Exhibition. From 1780-1836, the Royal Academy of Arts Summer Exhibition was held in the magnificent Great Room of Somerset House, in the Strand. Sir William Chambers designed this room to be densely hung from floor to ceiling with paintings, arranged in tiers according to the fashion of the French Salon. It was a matter of bitter rivalry among Academicians as to who was hung "above" and "below" the famous "line", the architectural moulding which formed a horizontal division around Chambers's room.

After the Royal Academy's move to Trafalgar Square (1836-1867) and then to Burlington House, in Piccadilly, great prestige was still attached to having one's picture

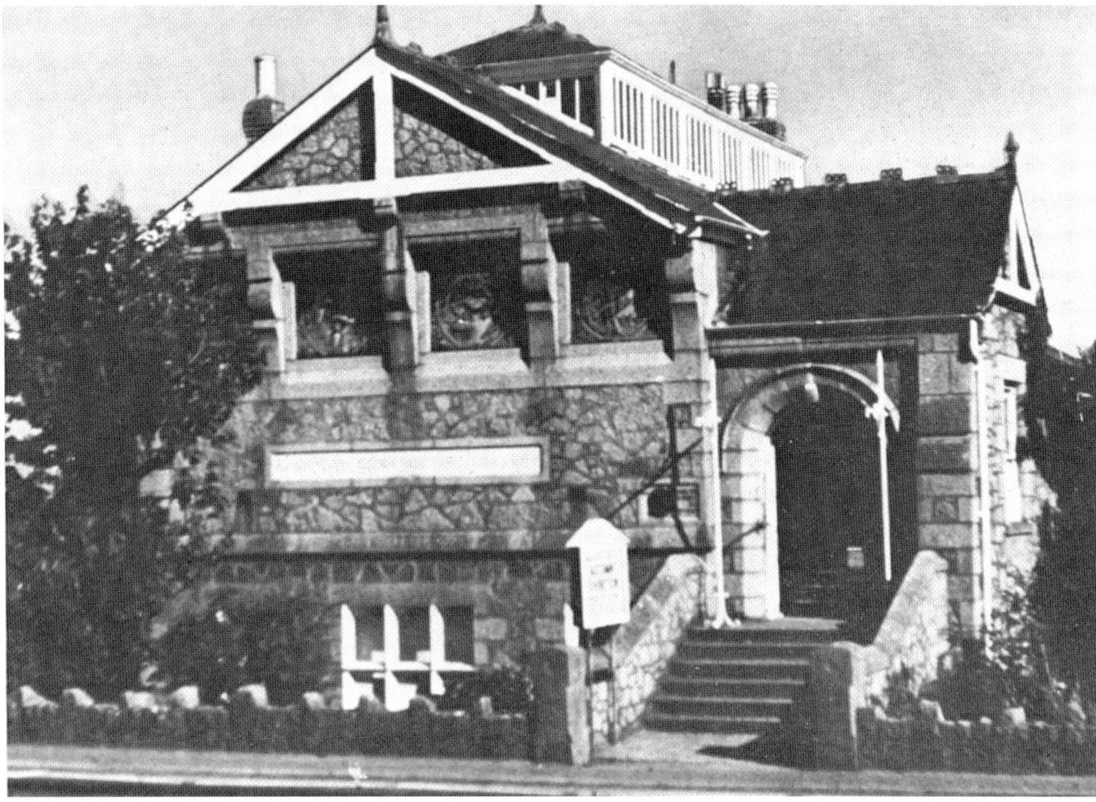

Newlyn Art Gallery

hung "on the line" (now an imaginary horizontal line level with the tops of the doors) so as to be in the most advantageous position for viewing.

Between 1904 and 1935 Frank Heath had 27 paintings accepted by the Royal Academy for their Summer Exhibition (see page 70), several of which were hung "on the line". For their journey up to London, they would have been packed into wooden crates and transported by train. In his younger days, Frank would have travelled up to the RA for 'varnishing day' to make any last minute alterations or additions to his pictures; it was also a great social occasion, meeting other artists and looking at their latest works.

During his time in Cornwall, he also exhibited 6 pictures at the Salon in Paris and 13 at the Liverpool Autumn Exhibition, held at the Walker Art Gallery (see page 71).

Generally before his marriage he signed his works FRANK HEATH; after 1910 he signed F. G. HEATH.

During the 1980s, with the resurgence of interest in pictures painted by artists of the "Newlyn School", several of Frank Heath's paintings were sold at various Auction Houses and at Art Galleries in London and around the country where they commanded good prices of up to £80,000.

Perhaps remembering what he had learnt from his student days at the Herkomer School in Bushey, Frank Heath also undertook a number of etchings.

Clapper Mill, situated at the top of the Lamorna Valley, dates back to the 15th century when it was called Trewoofe Mill and formed part of the de Trewoofe estates. In 1495, John and Isabella de Trewoofe had six daughters and no sons. They therefore decided to divide their property amongst their daughters and the mill was given to Alice and her

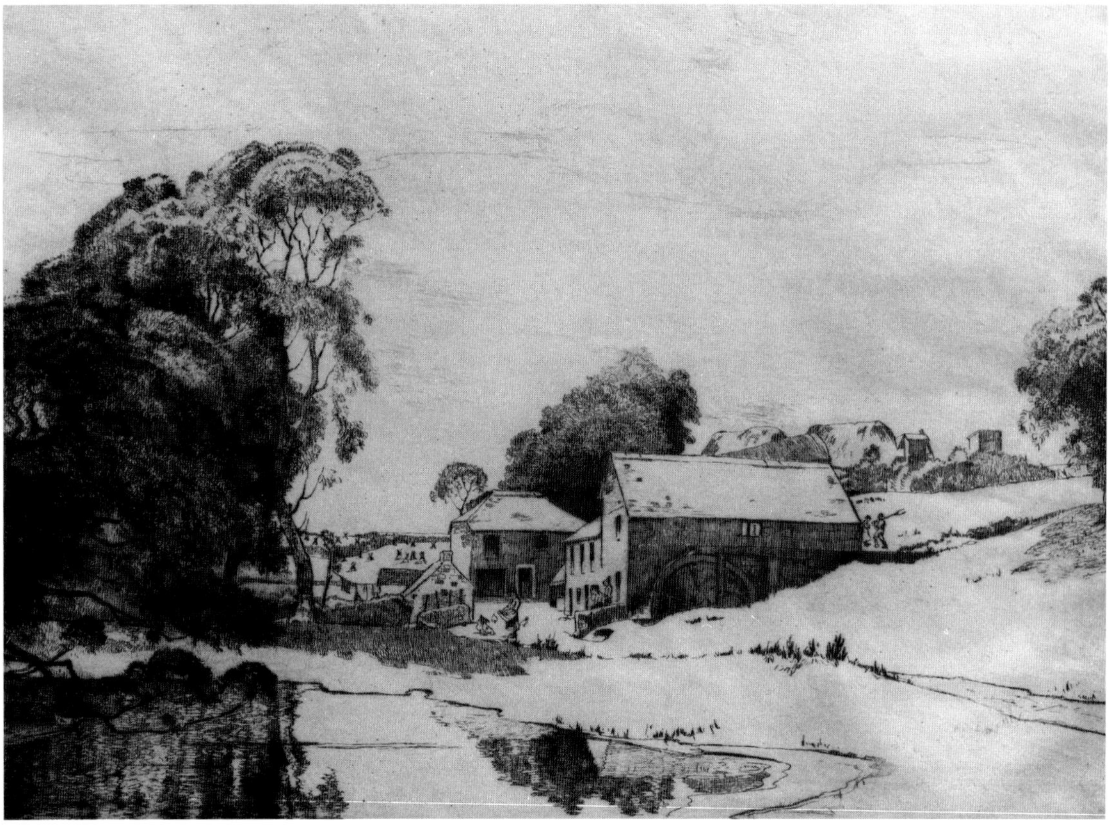

Clapper Mill by Frank Heath. Etching 10" x 14"

husband, Laurence Penkevell. Since then its ownership has changed many times. Clapper continued as a working mill until 1960, the last miller being Willie Clements. The mill has been painted by several Lamorna artists and there is a fine picture, "'January'. The mill at Lamorna", by Lamorna Birch in the Penzance and District Museum and Art Gallery.

At the centre of the de Trewoofe estates was the old medieval manor house, lived in by John and Hawais de Trewoofe around 1270. When John and Isabella divided their property in 1495, the manor house was given to another of their daughters, Joanna and her husband Thomas Lavelis. The family continued to live in the house until 1700 when, as there was no male heir, the two daughters sold it. The house was split into three properties but was allowed to deteriorate and very little of the original remains. Plate 29 of Trewoofe, painted by Frank Heath, shows the house as it was in the 1920s.

FRANK GASCOIGNE HEATH

1873 – 1936

"PICTURES AT AN EXHIBITION"

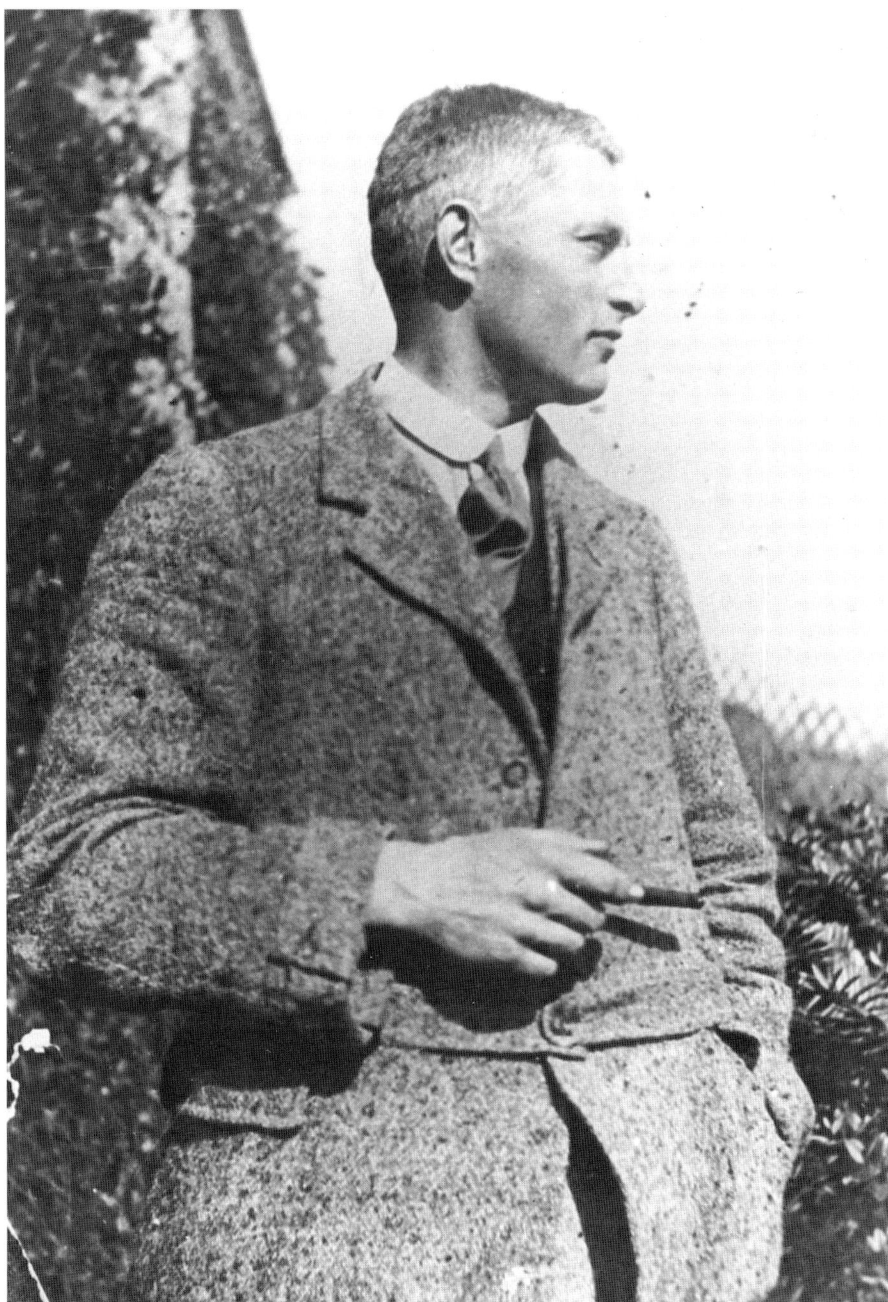

The Artist - circa 1910

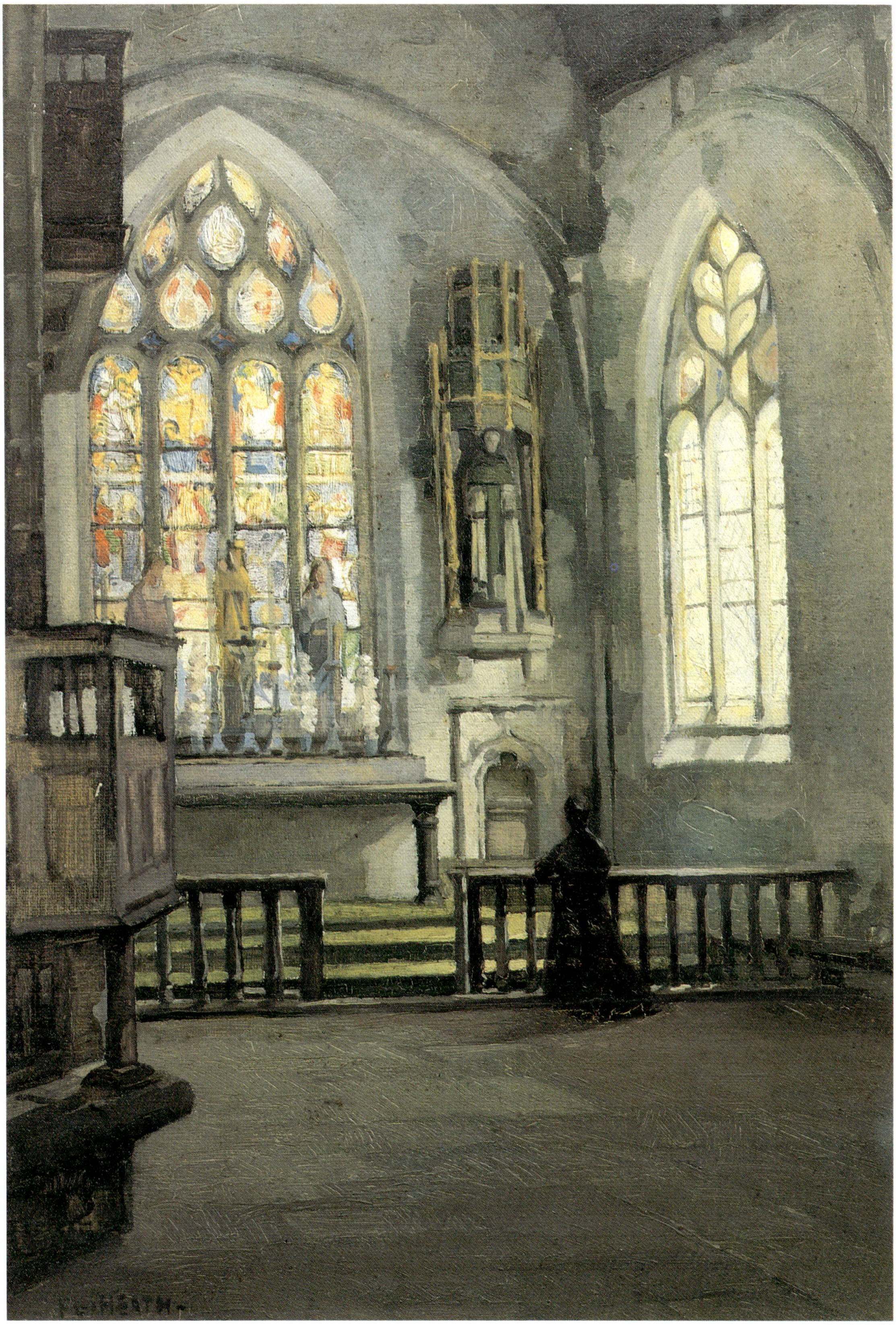

Plate 1 Interior of a Church at Louvain, Belgium Oil 14" x 10"
Painted while studying at the Academy of Fine Arts in Antwerp, 1895-1897.

The paintings below show the influence of Stanhope Forbes and the realism depicted by the first generation of Newlyn artists.

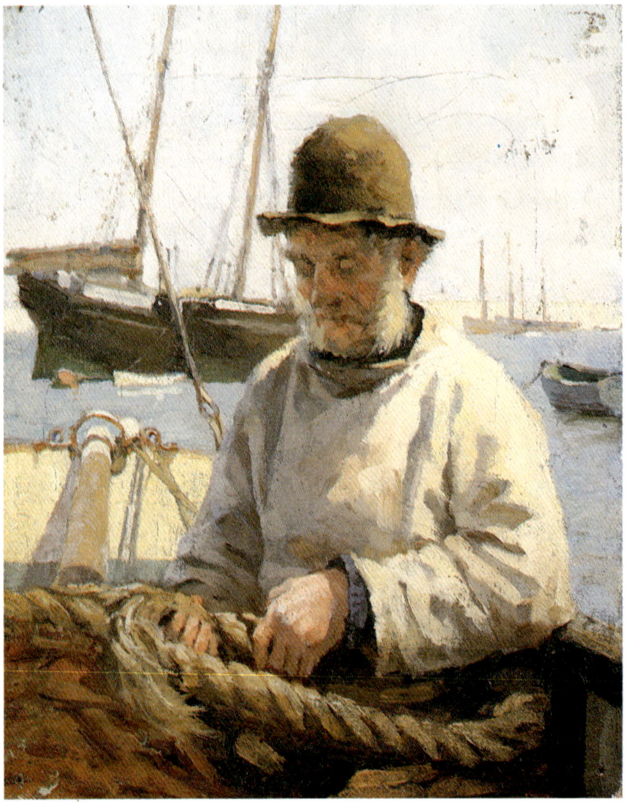

Plate 2

Study of an Old Fisherman

Oil 10" x 8"

David Messum Fine Art

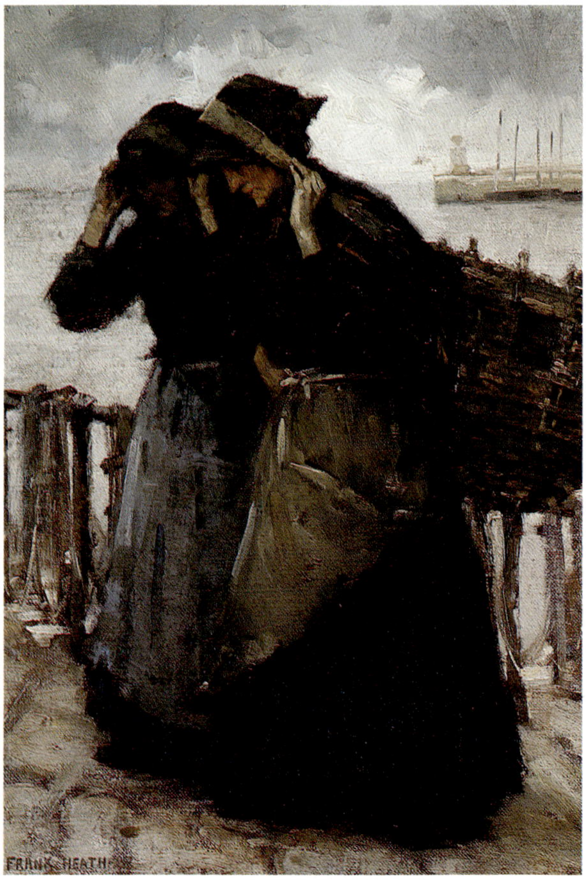

Plate 3

Fishwives with their Creels

Oil 18" x 12"

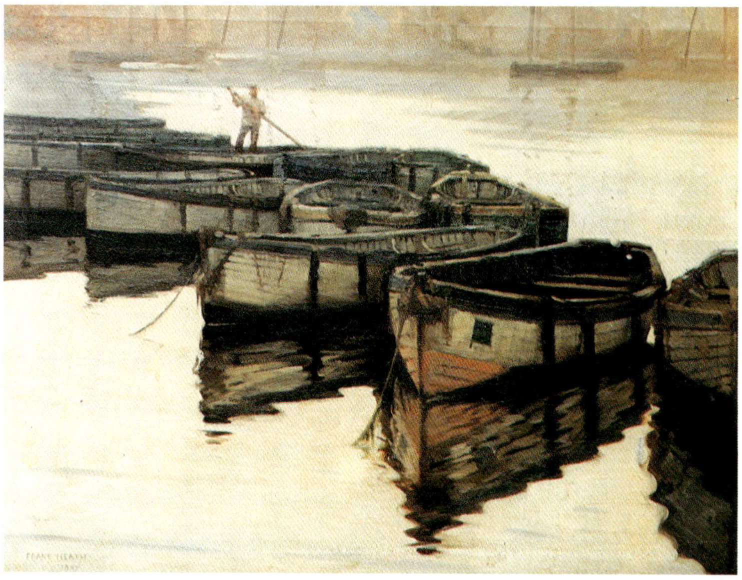

Plate 4 "Shoving Off" Oil 28" x 36"

Exhibited at the Royal Academy in 1907.

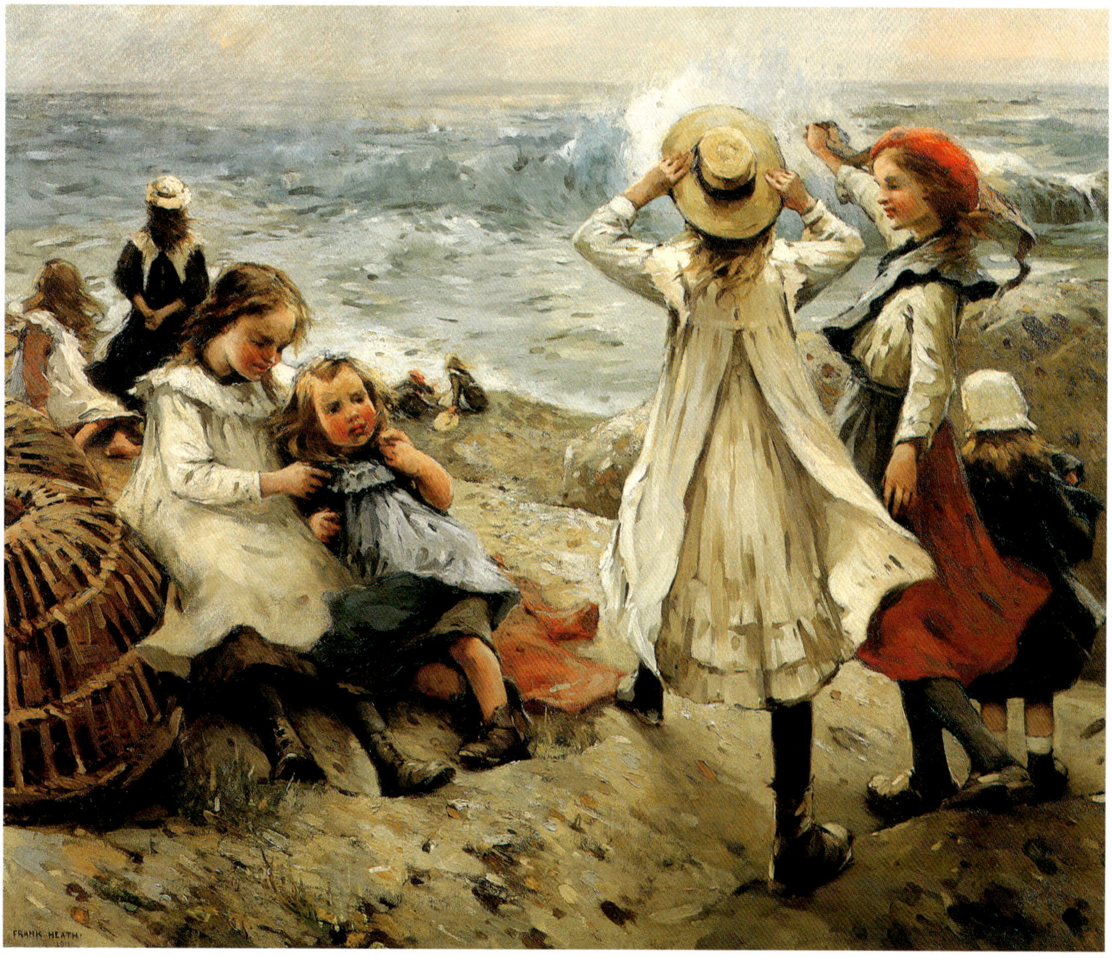

Plate 5 After the Storm Oil 50" x 60"

This painting was exhibited at the Royal Academy in 1911.
Richard Green, London

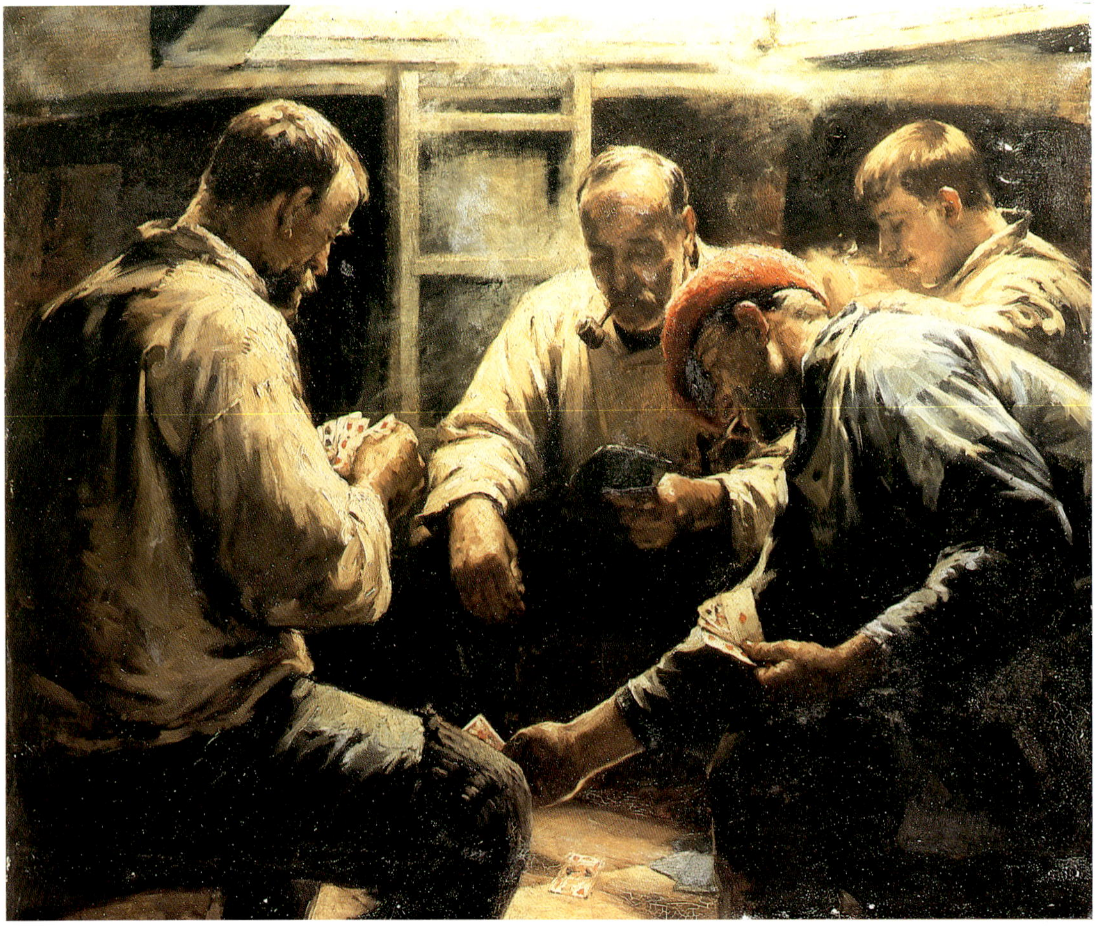

Plate 6 Cut Throat Euchre Oil 50" x 60"

Fishermen in their traditional smocks playing euchre in the hold of a boat. Exhibited at the Royal Academy in 1909.

Phillips Fine Art Auctioneers, London.

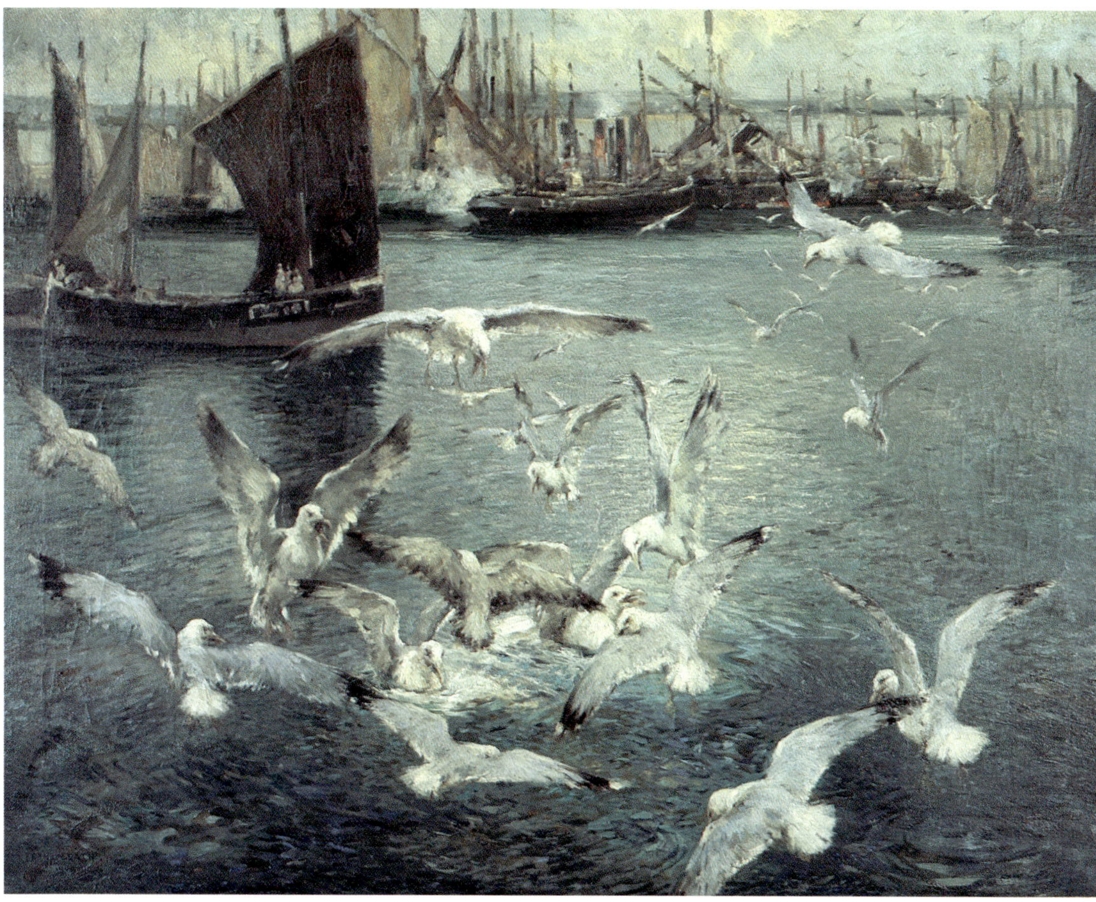

Plate 7 Sea-birds (Gulls in Newlyn Harbour) Oil 28" x 36"

Exhibited at the Walker Art Gallery in 1909 and the Royal Academy in 1911.

Royal Cornwall Museum, Truro.

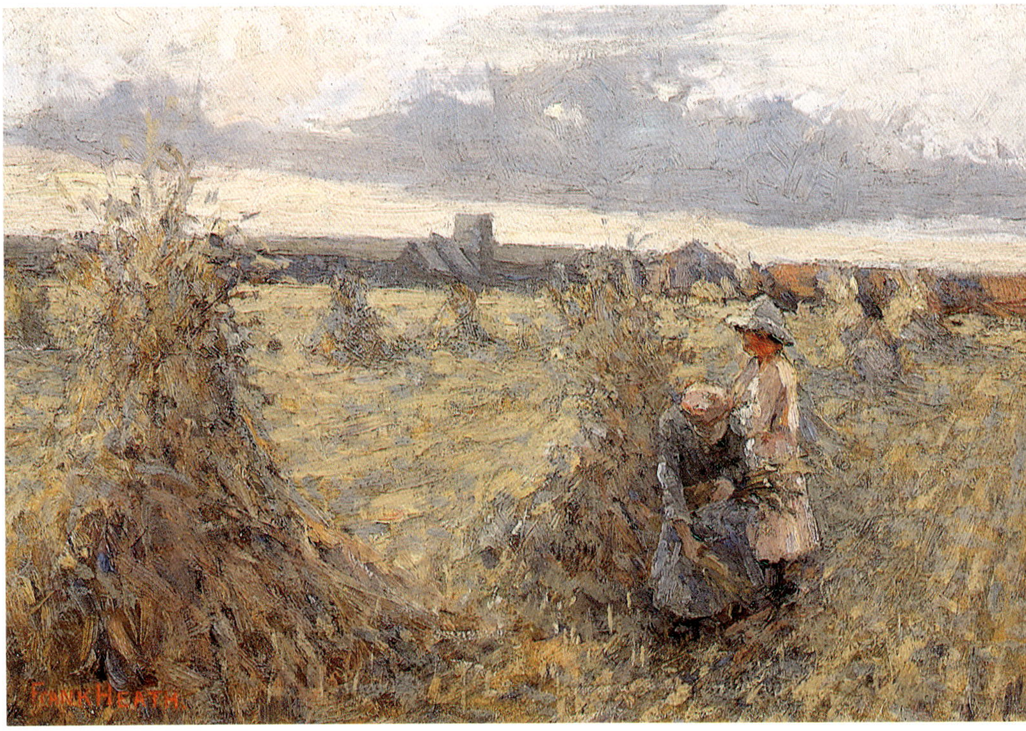

Plate 8 Corn Stooks Oil 9" x 14"

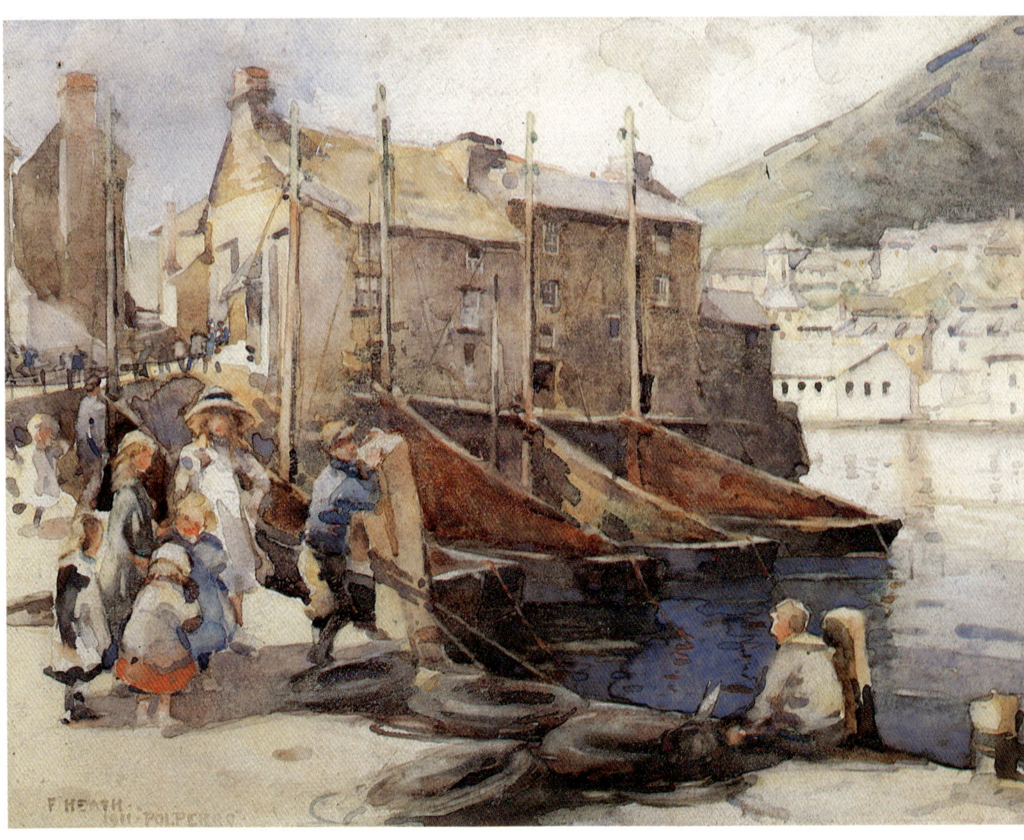

Plate 9 Polperro Watercolour 10" x 14"

This watercolour was used as a study for a large oil painting "Grey roofs beside a narrow wharf in cluster" (exhibited at the Walker Art Gallery in 1912.)

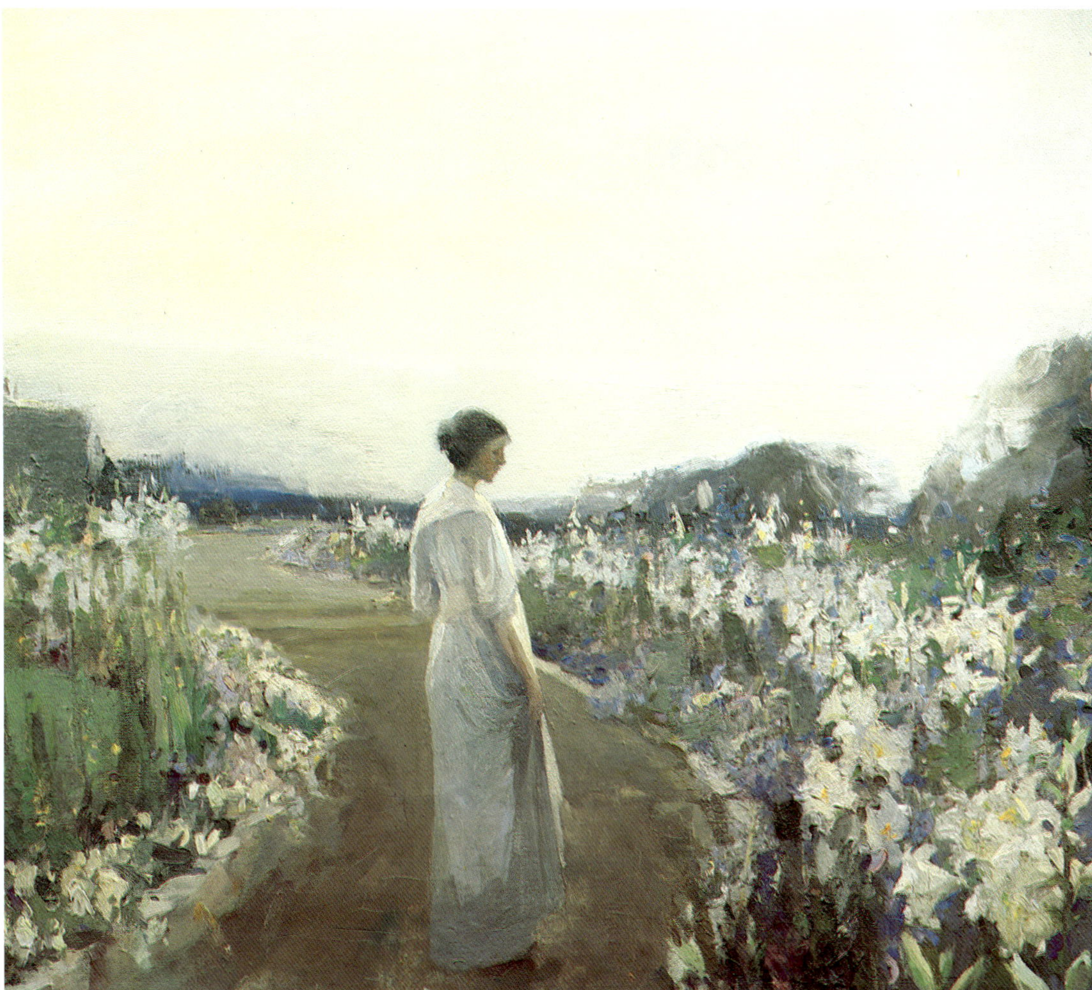

Plate 10 The Lily Border Oil 28" x 36"

Jessica in her garden at Menwinnion. Exhibited at the Newlyn Art Gallery in 1916.

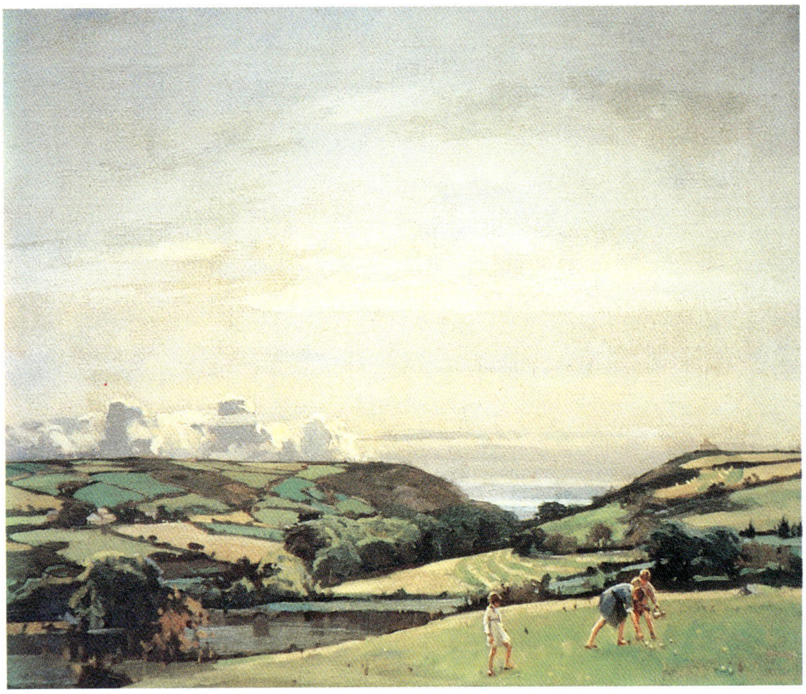

Plate 11 The Mushroom Pickers Oil 12" x 18"

Aileen, Tony and Gabriel in the fields above Lamorna.

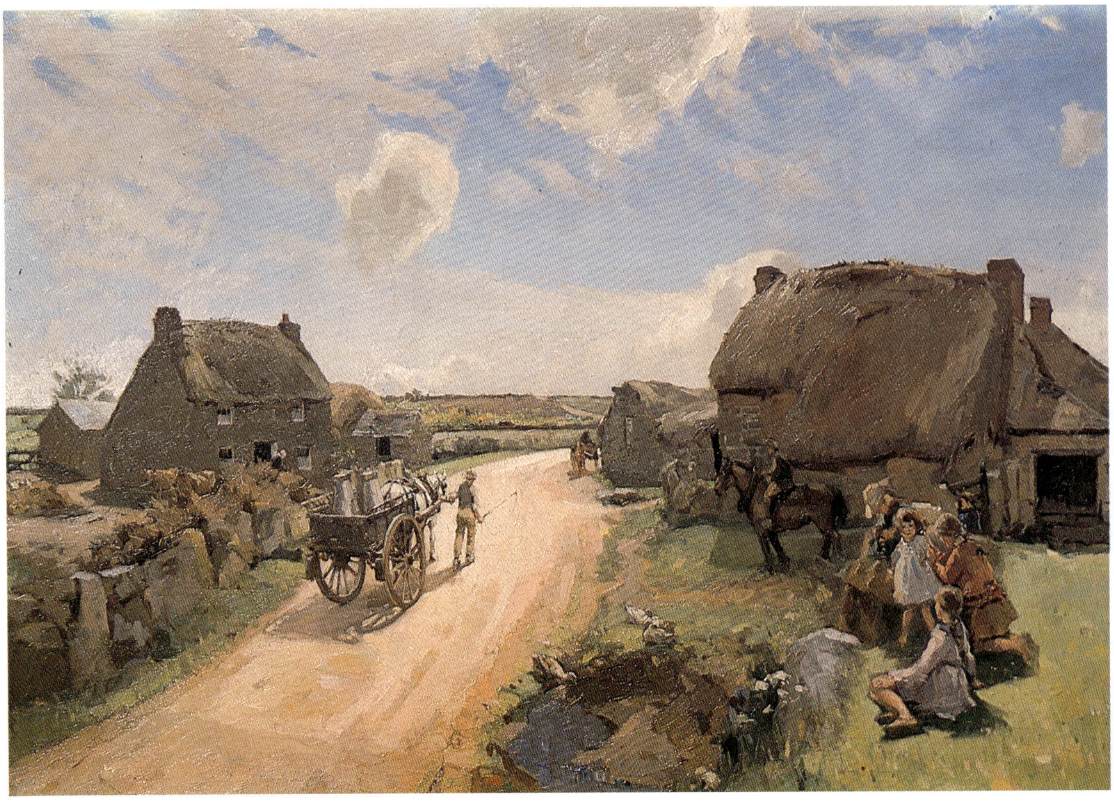

Plate 12 The Milk Cart Oil 40" x 60"

Approaching Boleigh Farm (see opposite). The Heath family can be seen in the bottom right of the picture.

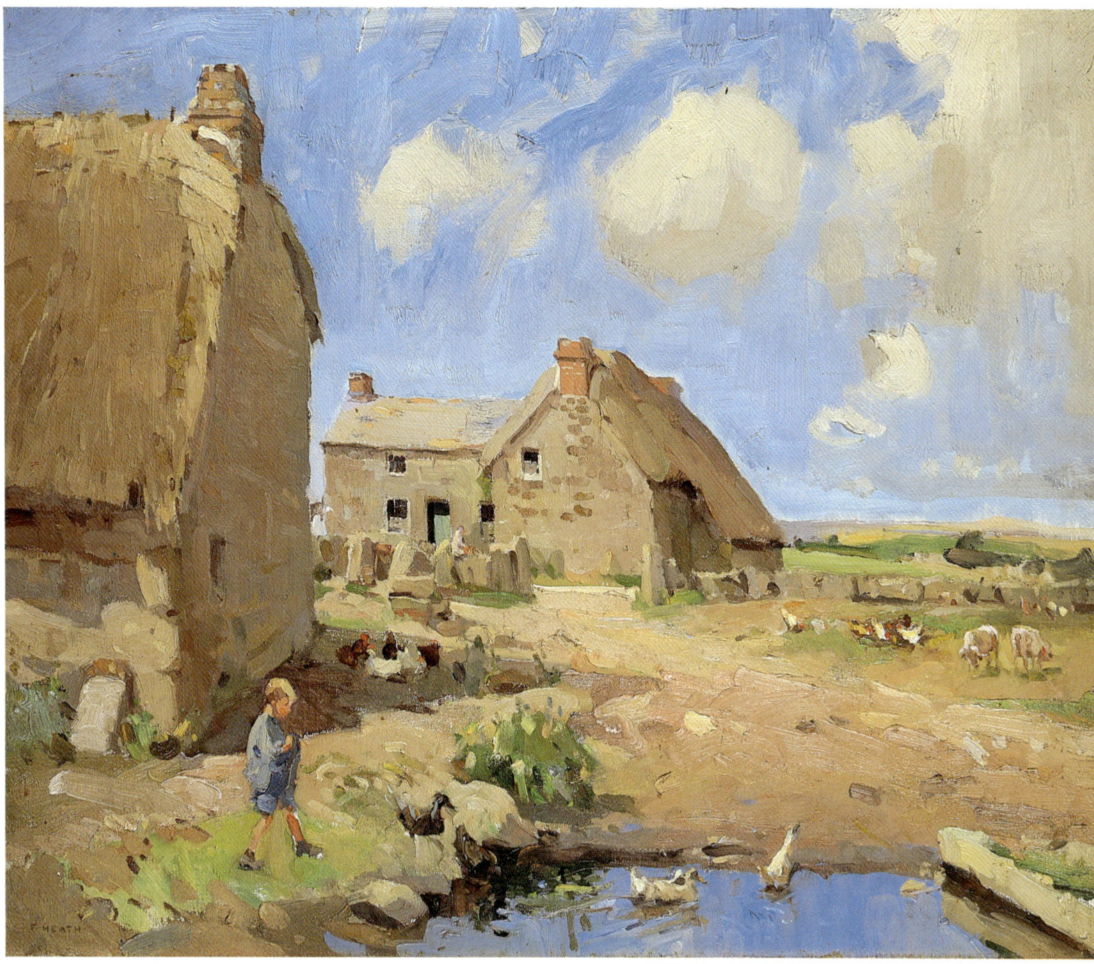

Plate 13 Boleigh Farm Oil 20" x 24"

Lamorna Birch, when he first arrived in Cornwall from Manchester around 1890, lodged at the farmhouse in the centre.

Phillips Fine Art Auctioneers, London.

Plates 14 and 15 show two aspects of the headland of Carn Barges, at Lamorna - by day and by night.

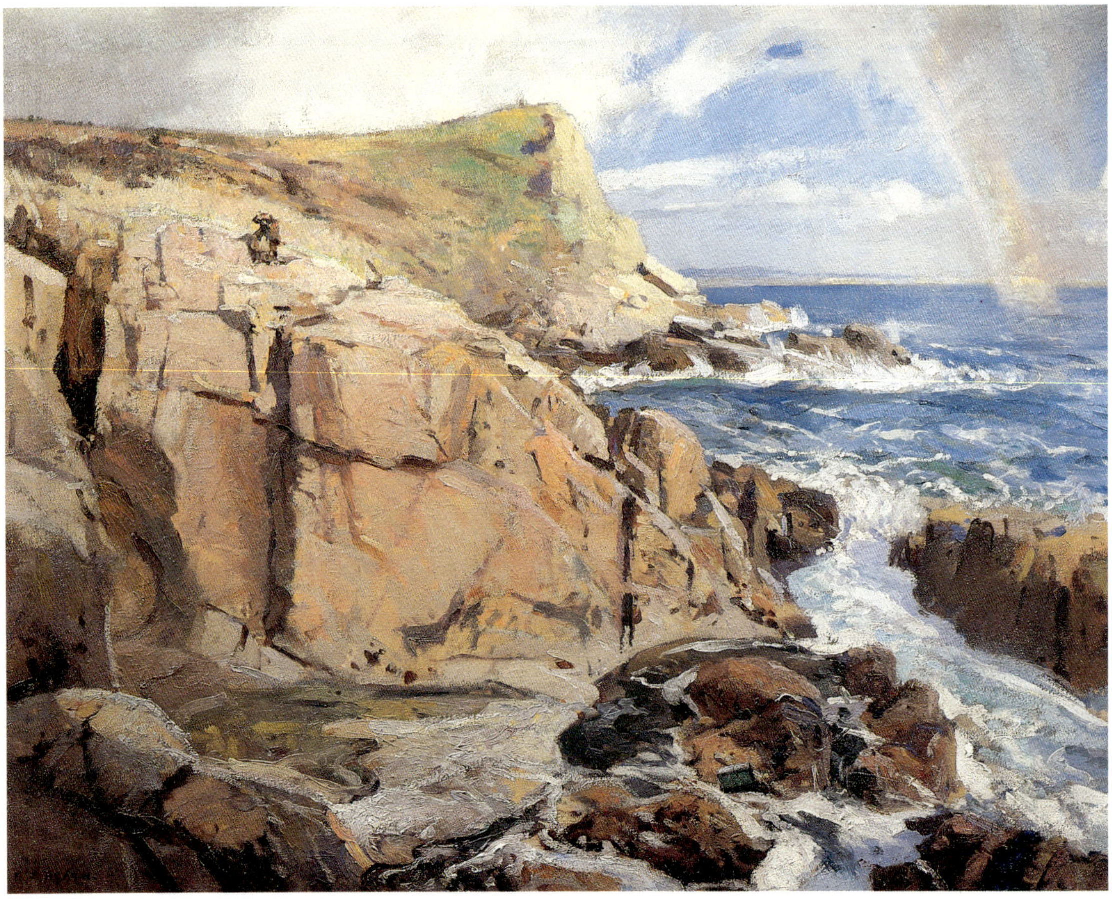

Plate 14 Carn Barges, Lamorna Oil 28" x 36"

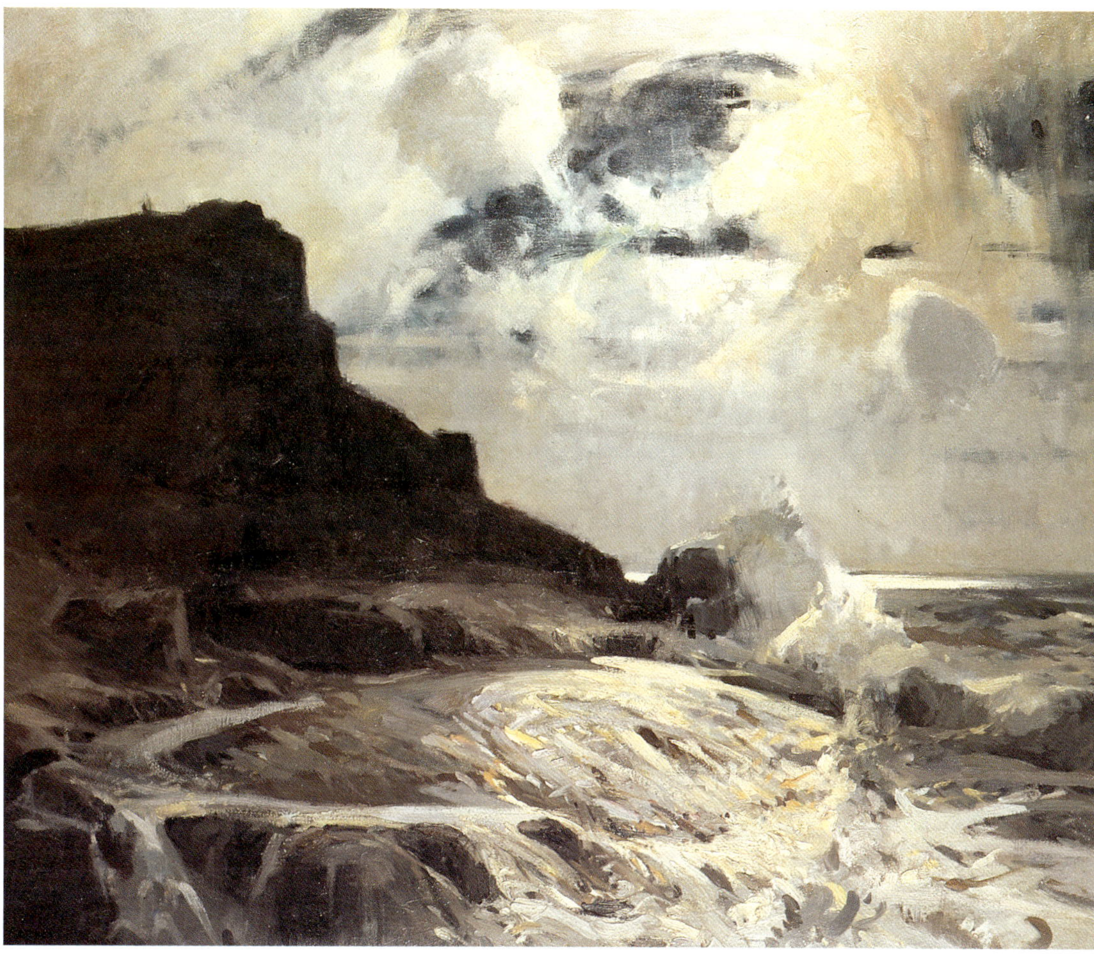

Plate 15 "There is music in the night" Oil 50" x 60"

Exhibited at the Royal Academy in 1922.

Phillips Fine Art Auctioneers, London.

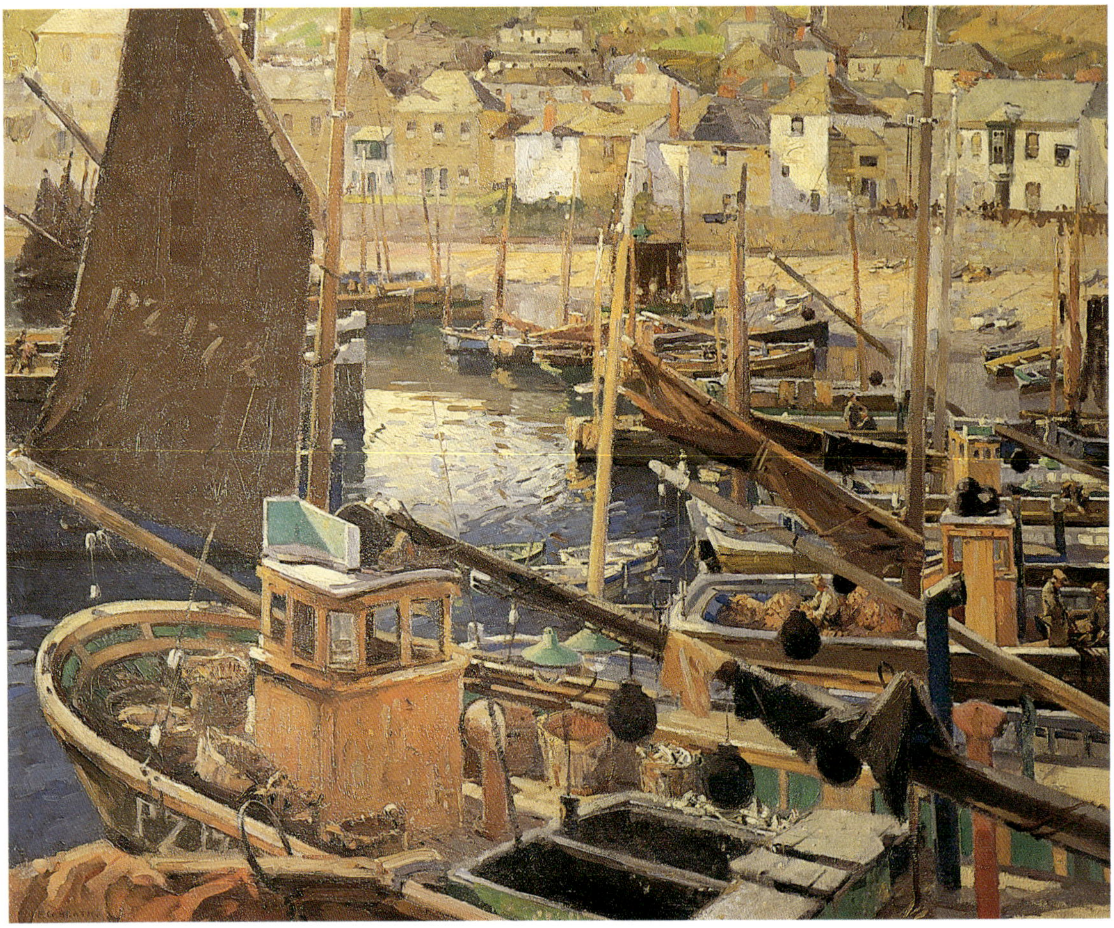

Plate 16 Saturday Morning in Harbour Oil 40" x 48"

Exhibited at the Royal Academy in 1922 and at the Salon in Paris in 1927 where it was awarded a "Mention Honorable" (as Mousehole Harbour, Cornwall). See page 72.

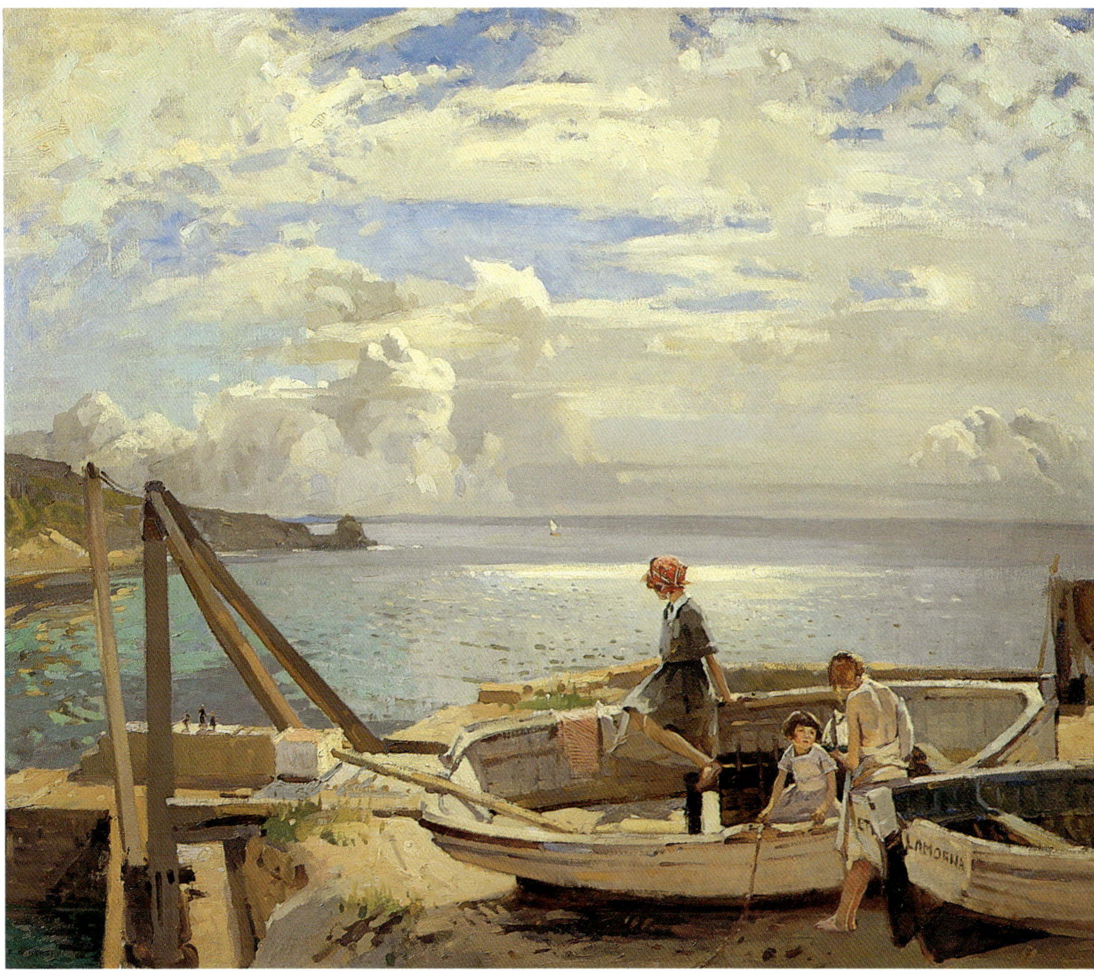

Plate 17 — Last Day of the Holidays — Oil 50" x 60"

Painted in 1922, this picture shows Frank Heath's three daughters, Aileen (in the red scarf), Gabriel (also in the boat) and Nancy at Lamorna Cove. It was exhibited at the Royal Academy in 1923.

Richard Green, London.

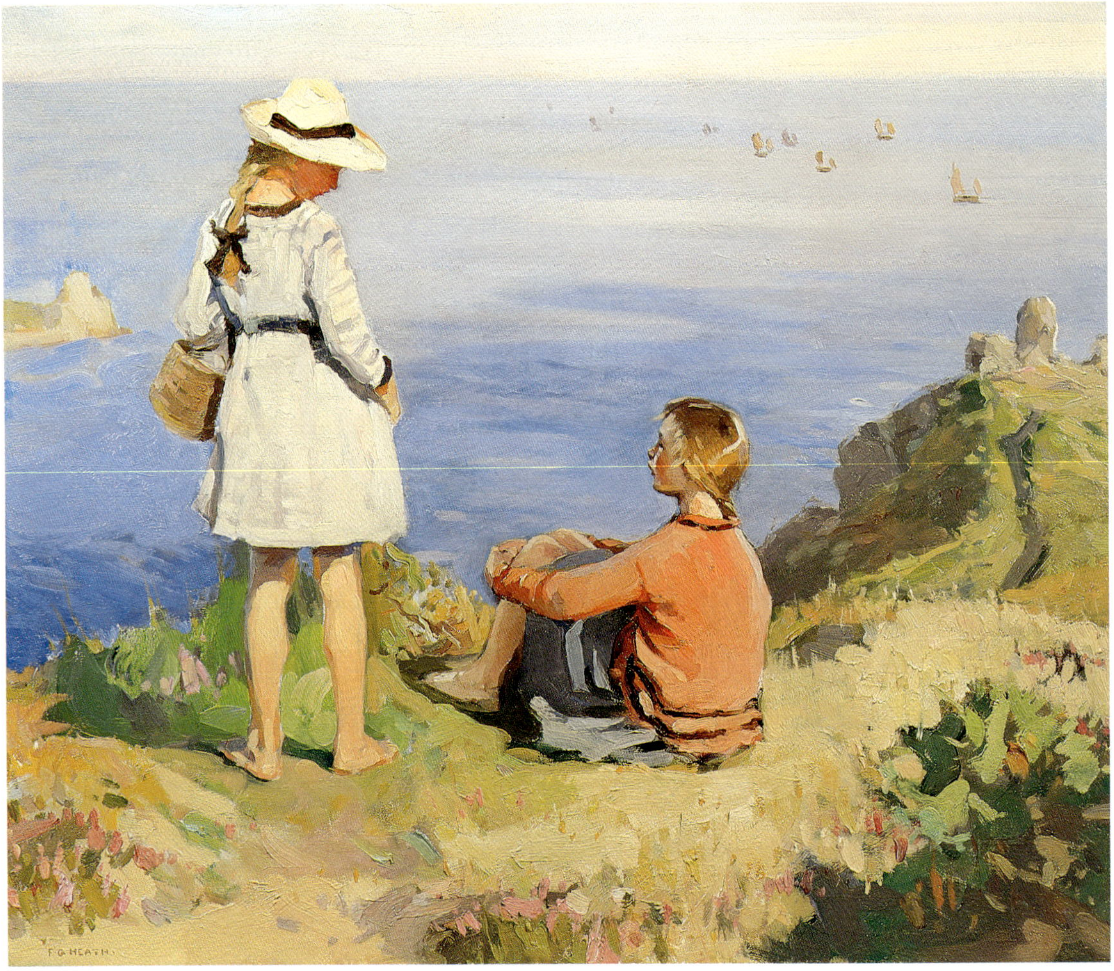

Plate 18 A Summer Afternoon Oil 20" x 24"

Aileen (left) and Nancy on the cliffs above Lamorna.

Richard Green, London.

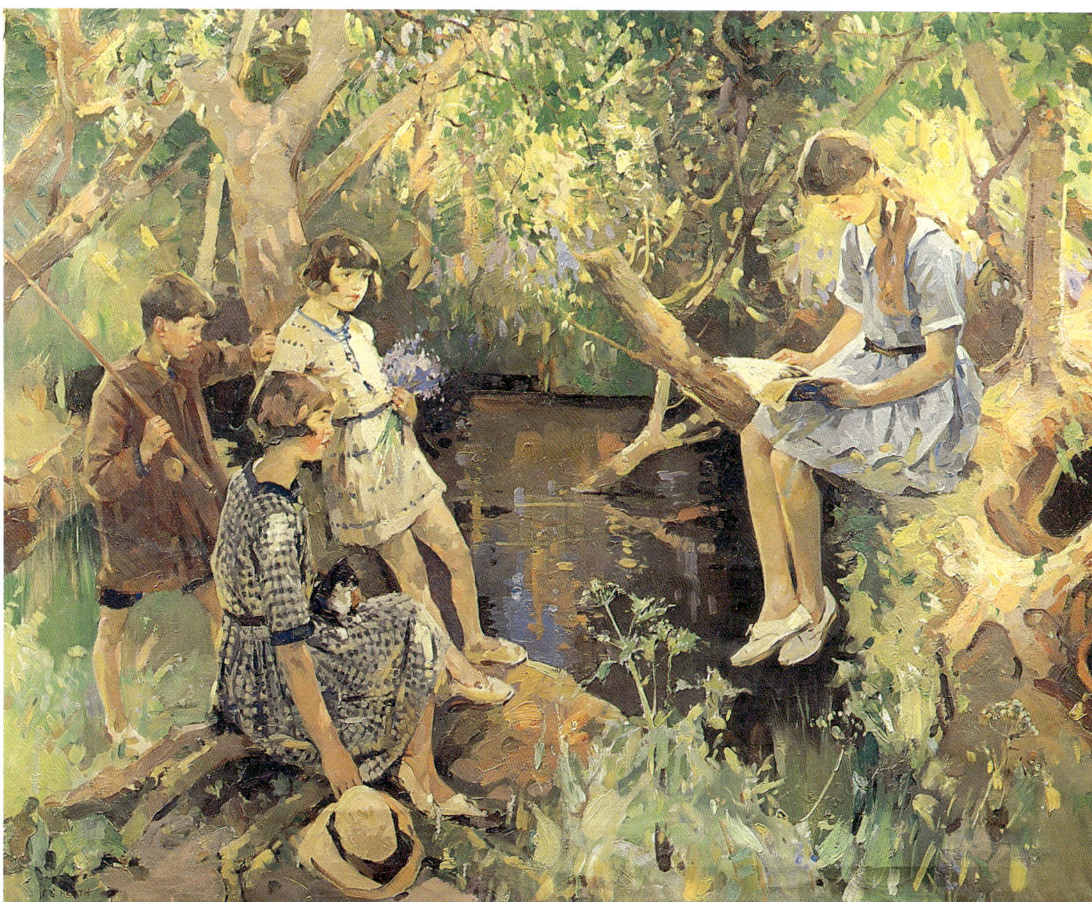

Plate 19 The Fairy Story Oil 40" x 50"

This picture, painted by the pond at the bottom of the garden at Menwinnion, shows Aileen (with Silko, the cat), Nancy (reading) and the twins Tony and Gabriel.

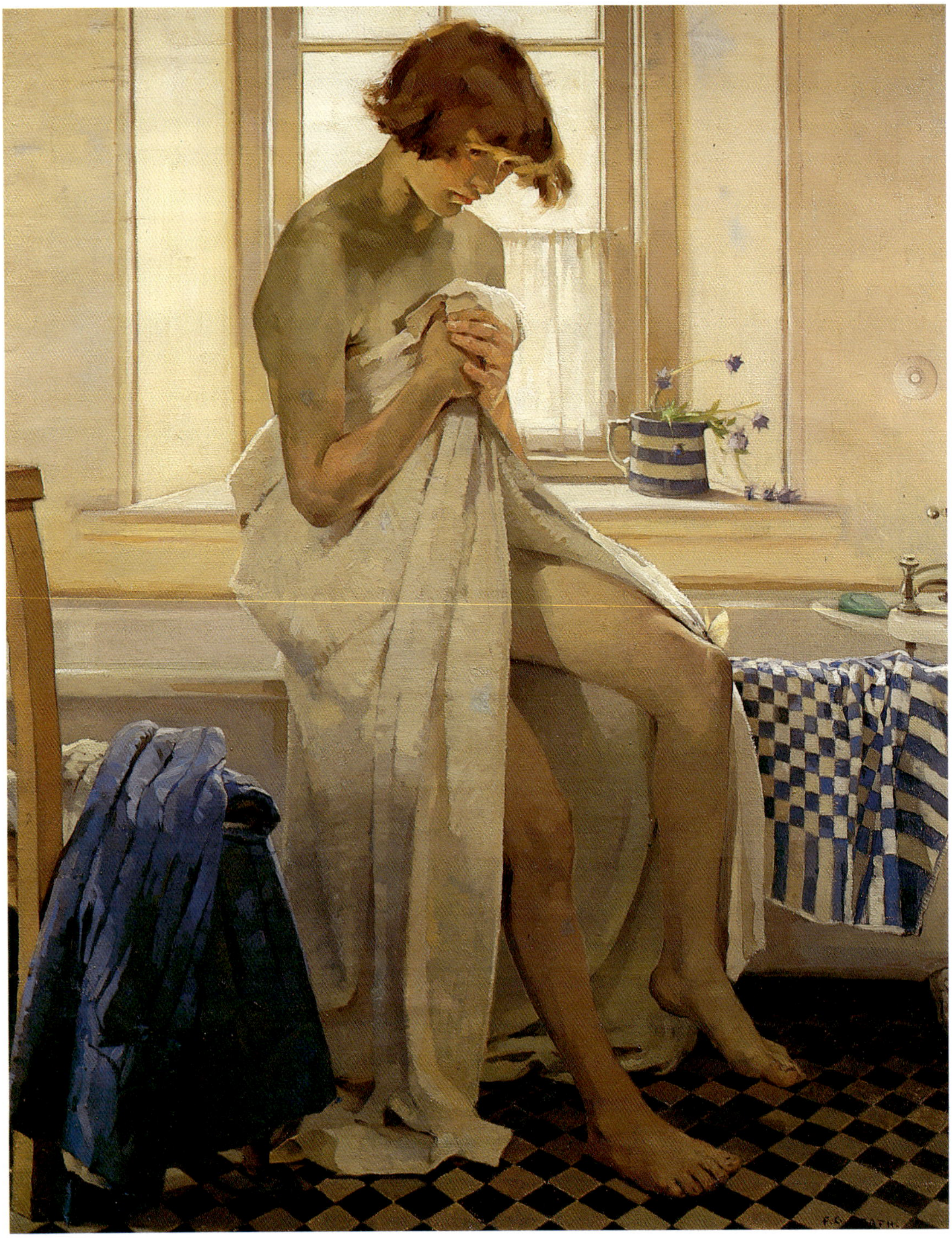

Plate 20 The Butterfly Oil 30" x 24"

Gabriel sitting on the side of the bath at Menwinnion with a butterfly settled on her knee. This picture was exhibited and hung "on the line" at the Royal Academy in 1928 and the Salon in Paris in 1930.

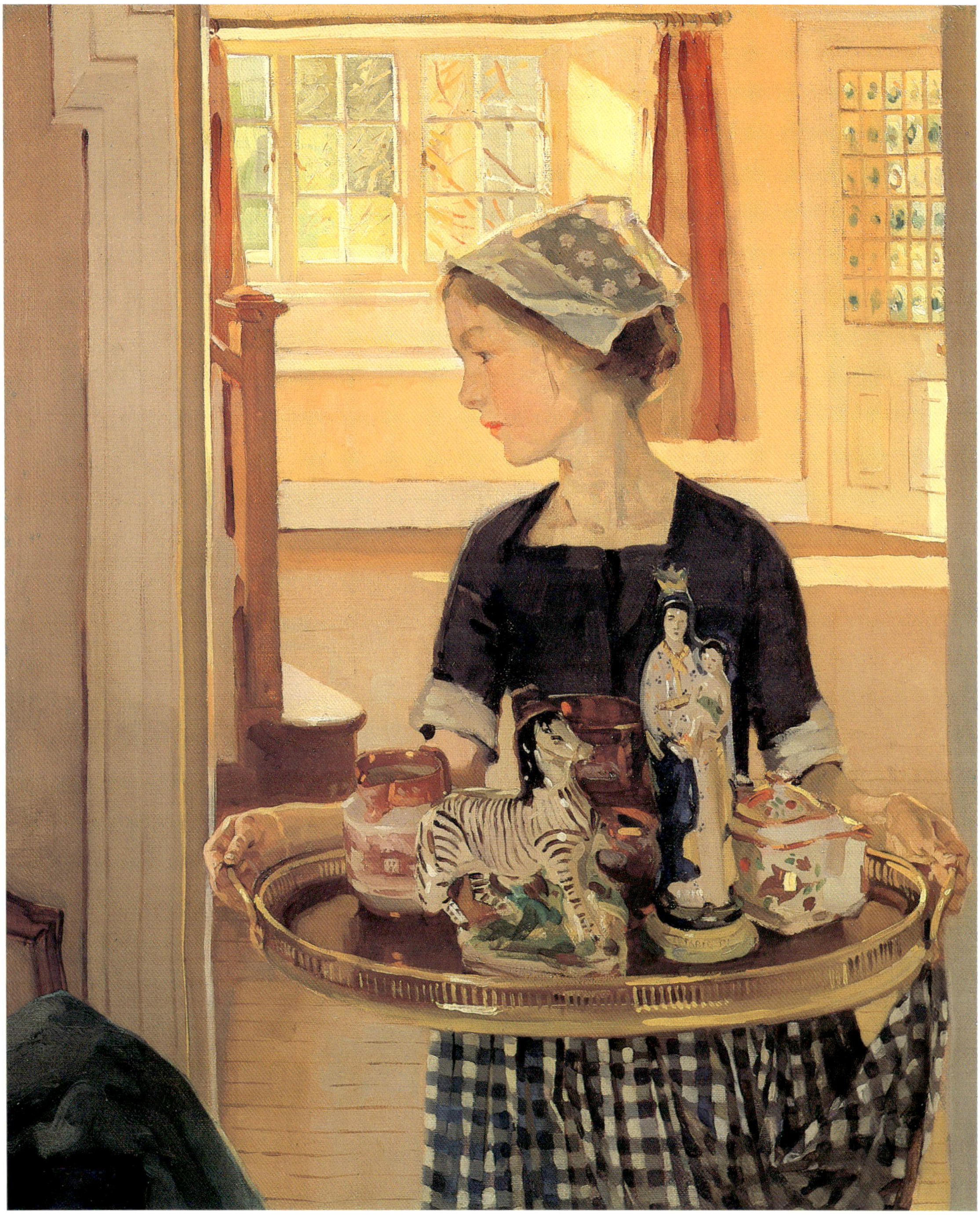

Plate 21 The Little Maid Oil 25" x 20"

Nancy, in the hall at Menwinnion. This picture was hung at the Royal Academy in 1923. It was also exhibited, in 1928, at a Gallery in Paris where one of the French reviewers wrote "Concerning the exhibition of a young maid carrying a tray loaded with porcelain whose smiling saucy face stands out against the yellow coloured panelling of a middle class room, the Englishman, Frank Heath has painted a small, charming picture. It is the type of British anecdote without any comment on life but at the same time not commonplace."

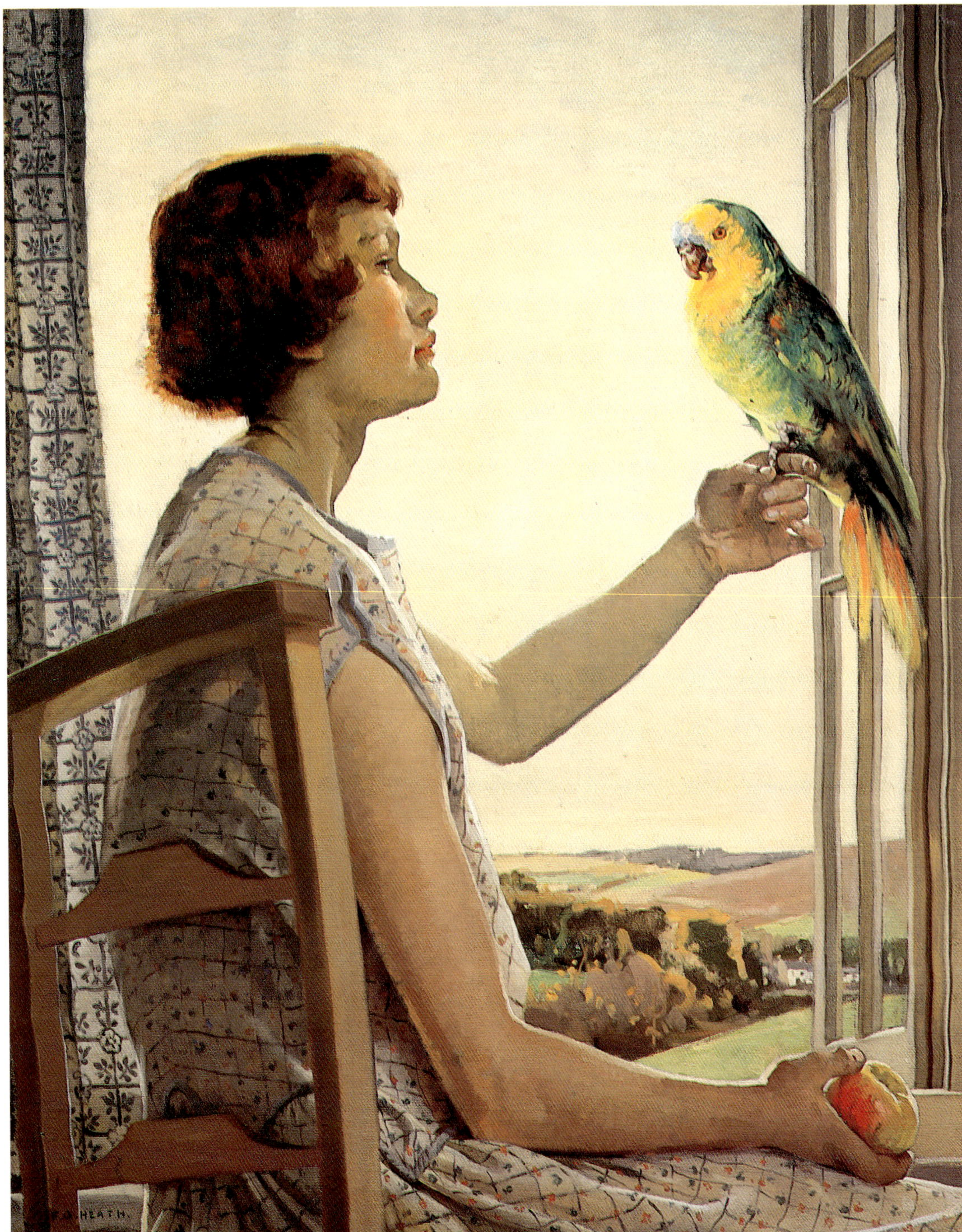

Plate 22 The Parrot Oil 30" x 24"

Gabriel with a parrot.

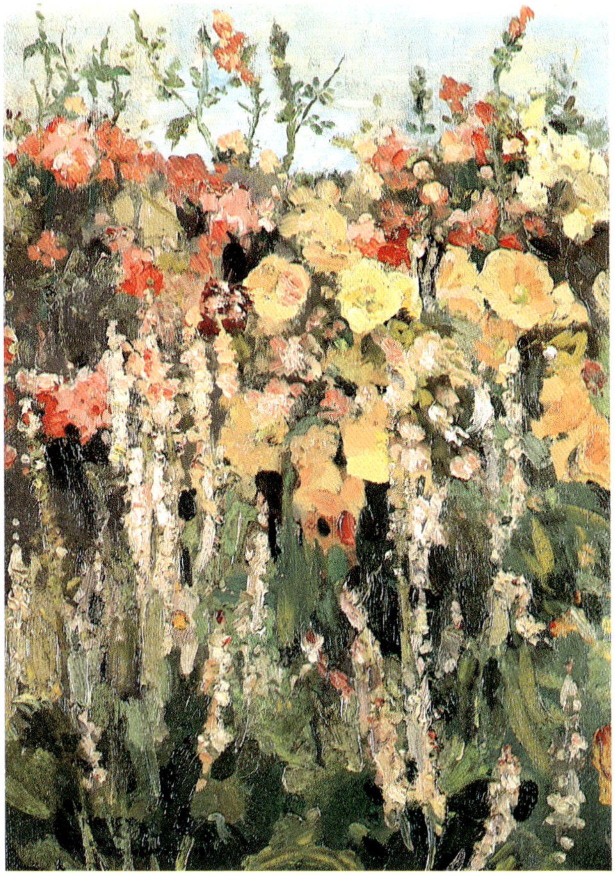

Plate 23

Hollyhocks

Oil 14" x 10"

Galerie Dobiaschofsky, Berne

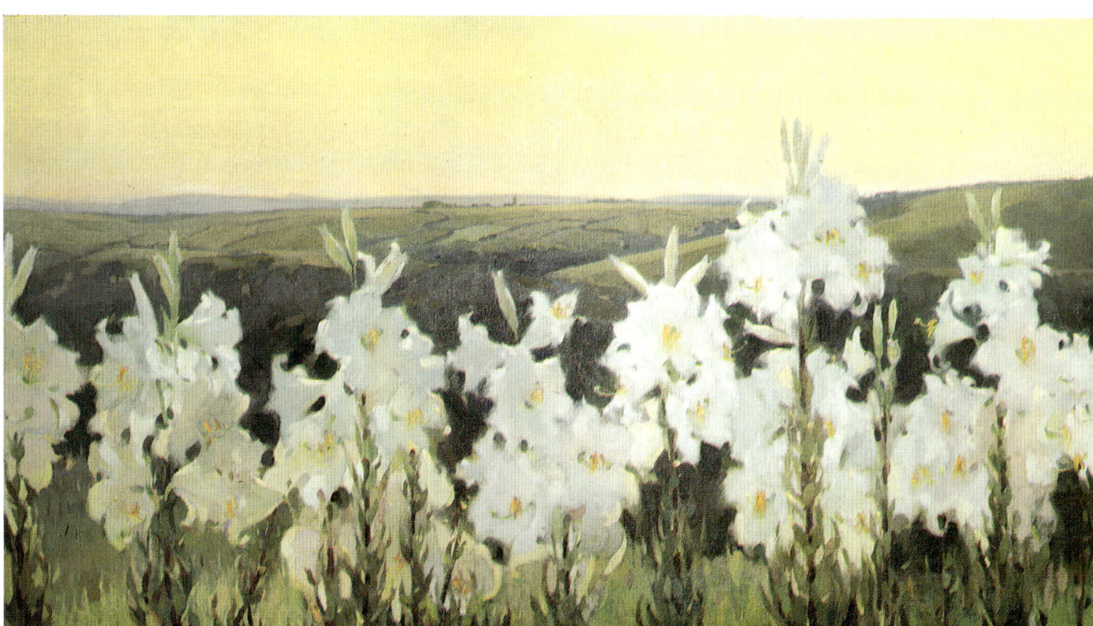

Plate 24 Madonna Lilies Oil 30" x 54"

Painted in the artist's garden at Menwinnion. This picture was exhibited at the Walker Art Gallery in 1929 and the Royal Academy in 1930. (See also cover.)

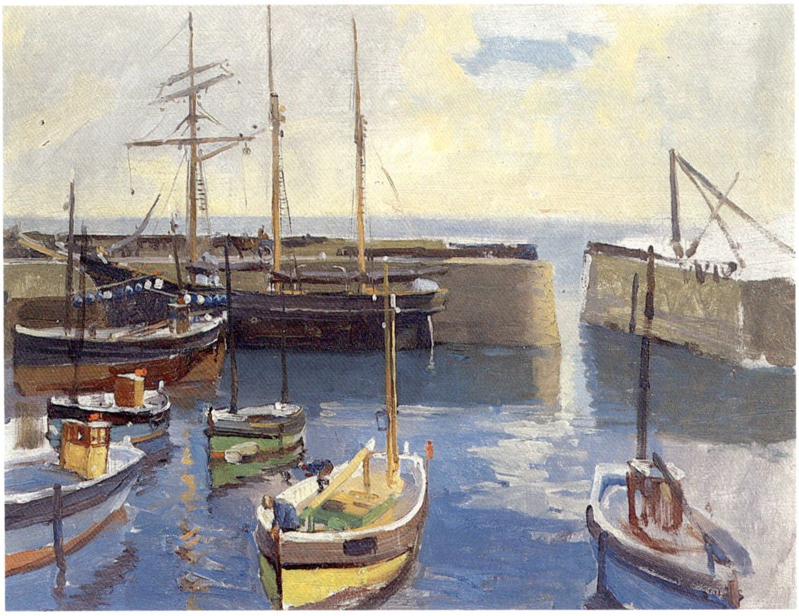

Plate 25 | Fishing Boats in Harbour | Oil 15" x 18"

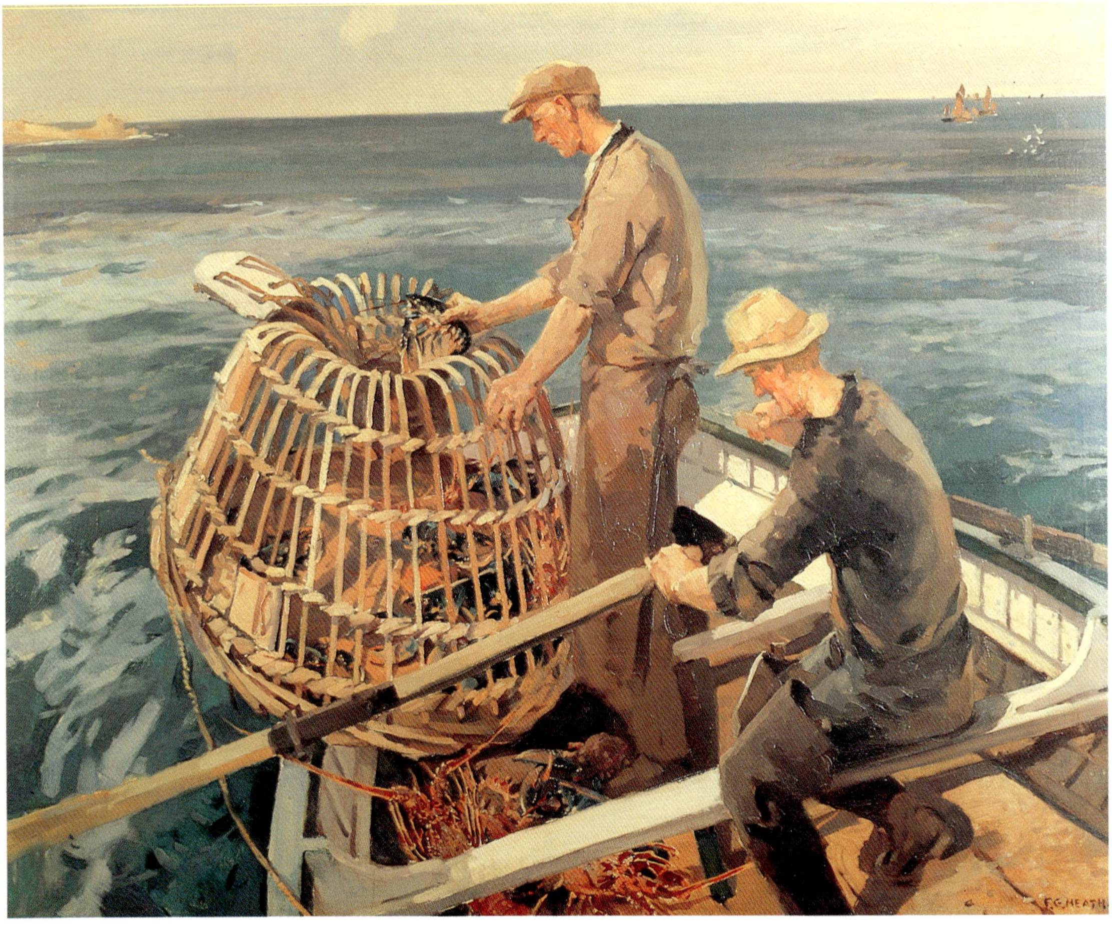

Plate 26 | The Store Pot | Oil 40" x 50"

Ben Jeffery (rowing) and Mr Whiting fishing off Lamorna. This picture was exhibited at the Salon in Paris in 1928 and now hangs in the Queens Hotel in Penzance.

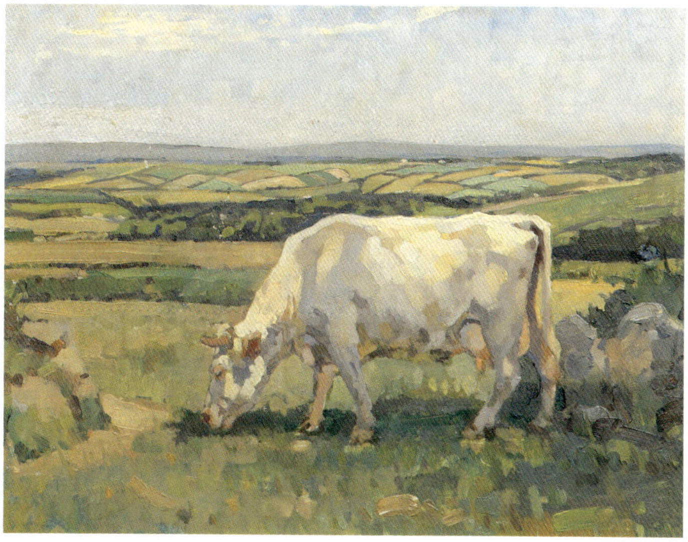

Plate 27 | The White Cow | Oil 9" x 12"

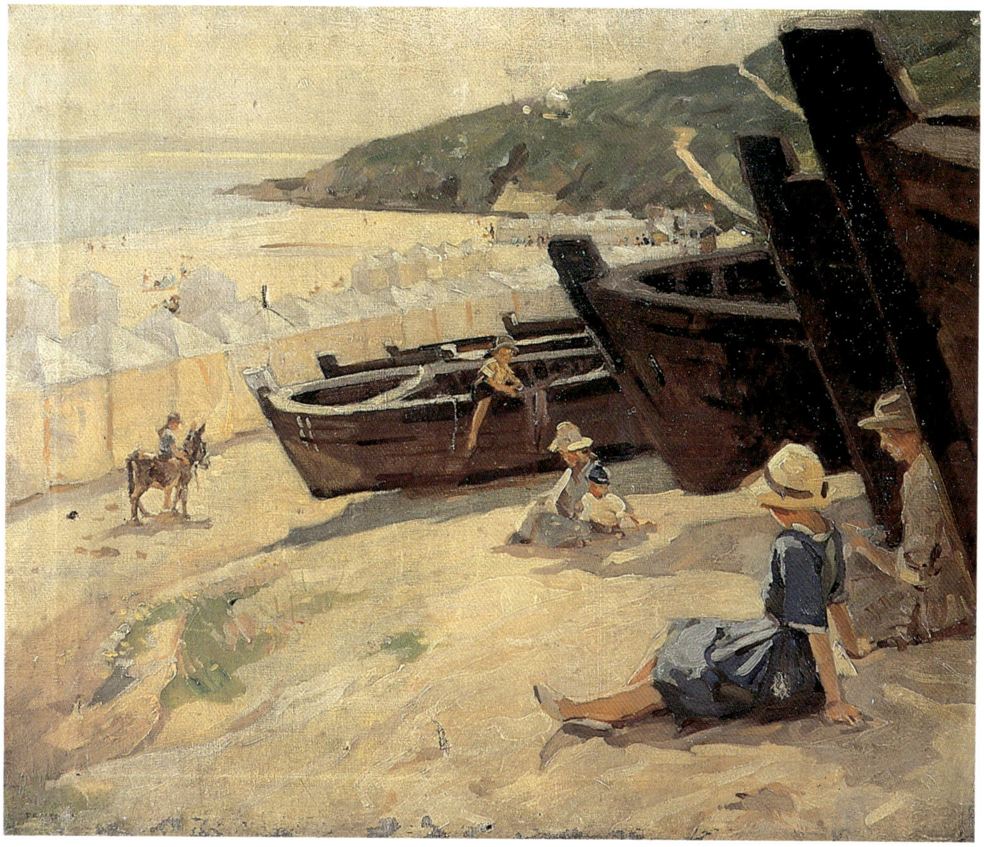

Plate 28 | Oil 20" x 24"

A family holiday at Porthminster beach, near St Ives in the 1920s. Gabriel is sitting on the donkey, Tony is playing on the boat, Aileen is in the blue dress and Jessica is knitting. In the top right hand corner can be seen smoke from the train as it steamed in to St Ives from St Erth.

Phillips Fine Art Auctioneers, London.

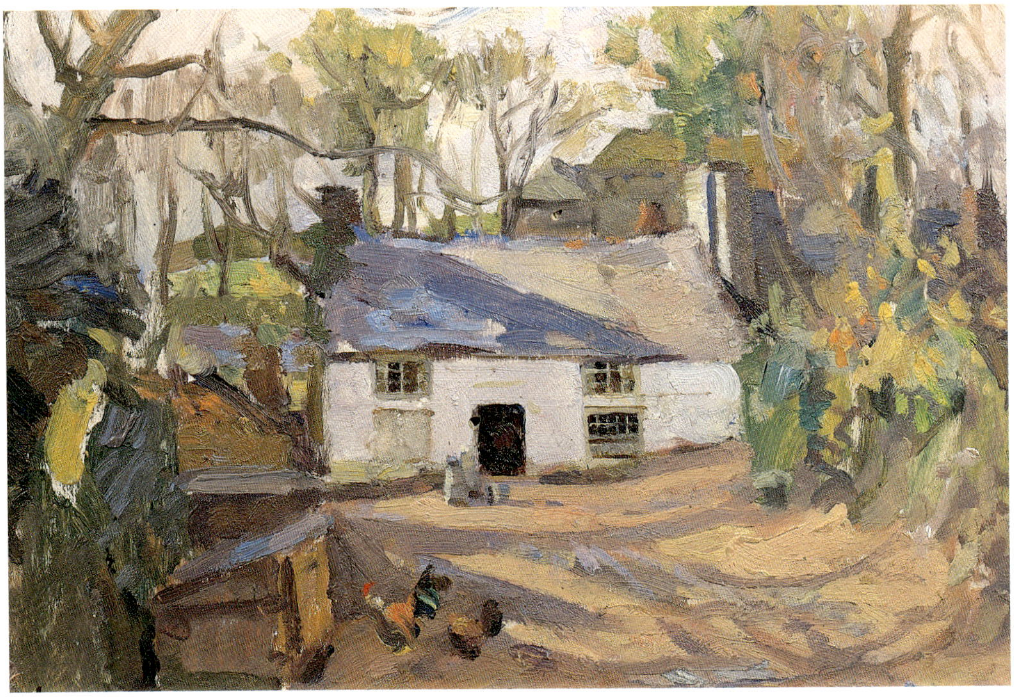

Plate 29 Trewoofe Oil 6" x 12"

Lamorna's oldest house. (See page 42.)

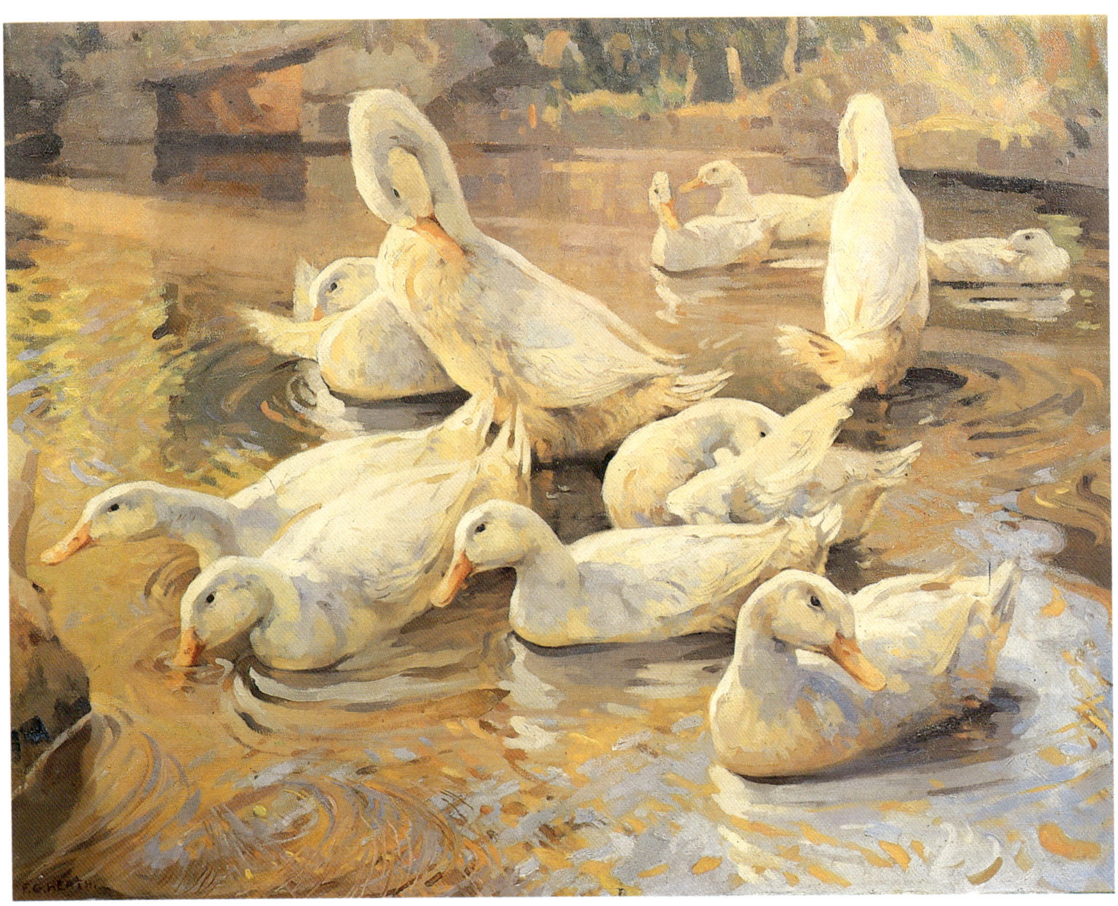

Plate 30 White Ducks at Lamorna Mill Oil 28" x 36"

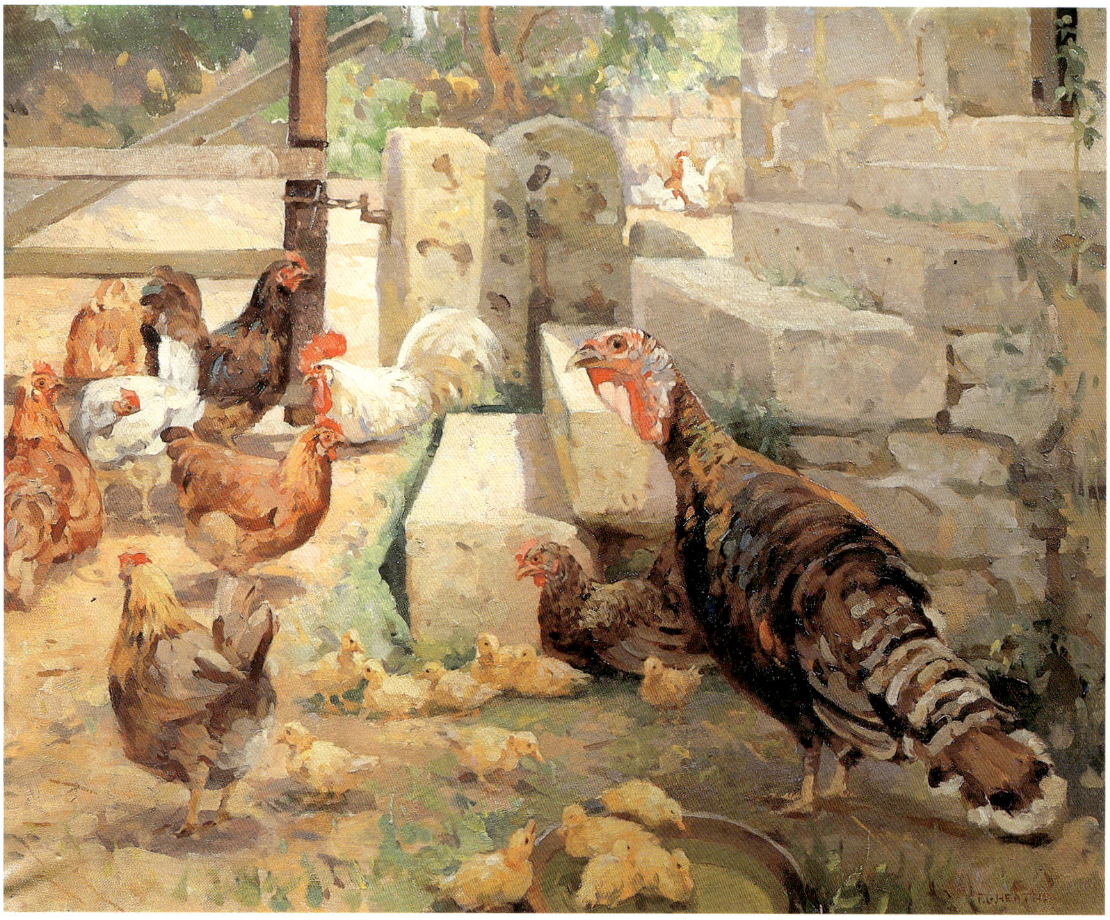

Plate 31 The Farmyard, Trewoofe Oil 24" x 30"

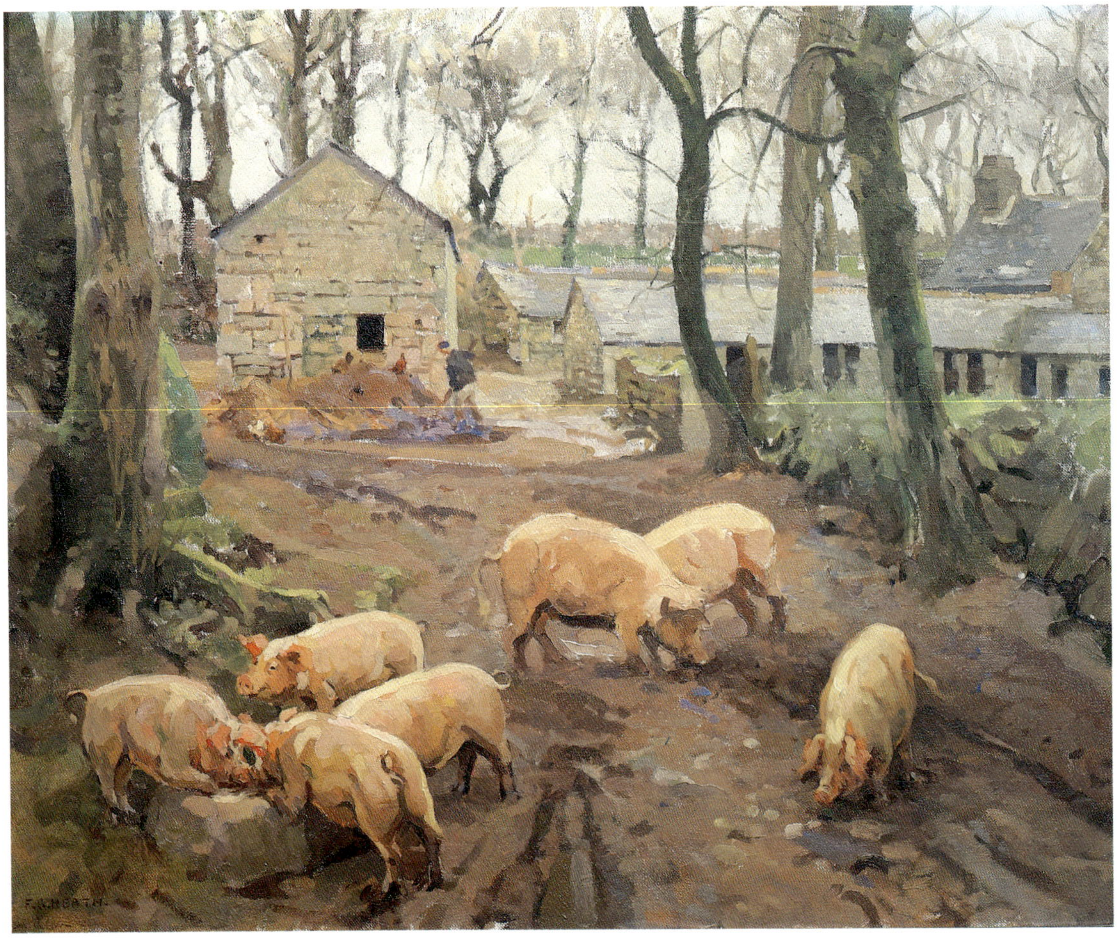

Plate 32 The Road to the Farm Oil 24" x 30"

Exhibited at the Royal Academy in 1935. Trewoofe Farm and its animals were popular subjects for several of the Lamorna artists. (See page 78.)

A List of paintings by Frank Heath hung at the Royal Academy of Arts, London for their Summer Exhibition.

1904	A Violin Solo
1905	Homeward
1906	His First Voyage
1907	Shoving Off
1909	Cut-throat Euchre
1911	Sea-birds Crumplehorn Mill After the Storm
1912	Old age Pensioners Jenifer
1913	"Calm on the seas and silver sleep." A Cottage Interior Mother and Child
1914	Stories of the Gun The Morning Room
1915	Amateur Gardeners
1916	The Fish Quay
1917	The Daisy Chain
1922	"There is music in the night" Saturday Morning in Harbour
1923	The Little Maid Last Day of the Holidays
1927	Nancy
1928	The Butterfly
1930	Madonna Lilies Girl Cleaning Kettle
1935	The Road to the Farm

A list of paintings by Frank Heath hung at the Salon in Paris.

1927	Mousehole Harbour, Cornwall Along the Cornish Coast
1928	The Store Pot
1929	A Cornish Farmyard Carn Barges (Cornwall)
1930	The Butterfly

A list of paintings by Frank Heath hung at the Walker Art Gallery, Liverpool for their Autumn Exhibition.

1903	The Fortune Teller	£52.10.0
1904	A Violin Solo	£21
1906	A Broken Melody	£30
1907	"Below in the valley there lies the world"	
1908	Come Michaelmas	£35
1909	Sea-birds	£52.10.0
1912	"The gentleness of heaven is upon the sea"	£52.10.0
	"Grey roofs beside a narrow wharf in cluster"	£150
1913	Jenifer	£52.10.0
	"Calm on the seas and silver sleep"	£150
1926	The Rehearsal	£20
1928	The Green Frock	£42
1929	Madonna Lilies	£40

Certificate from the Salon in Paris, presented to Frank Heath in 1927, for his picture of Mousehole Harbour. (Plate 16)

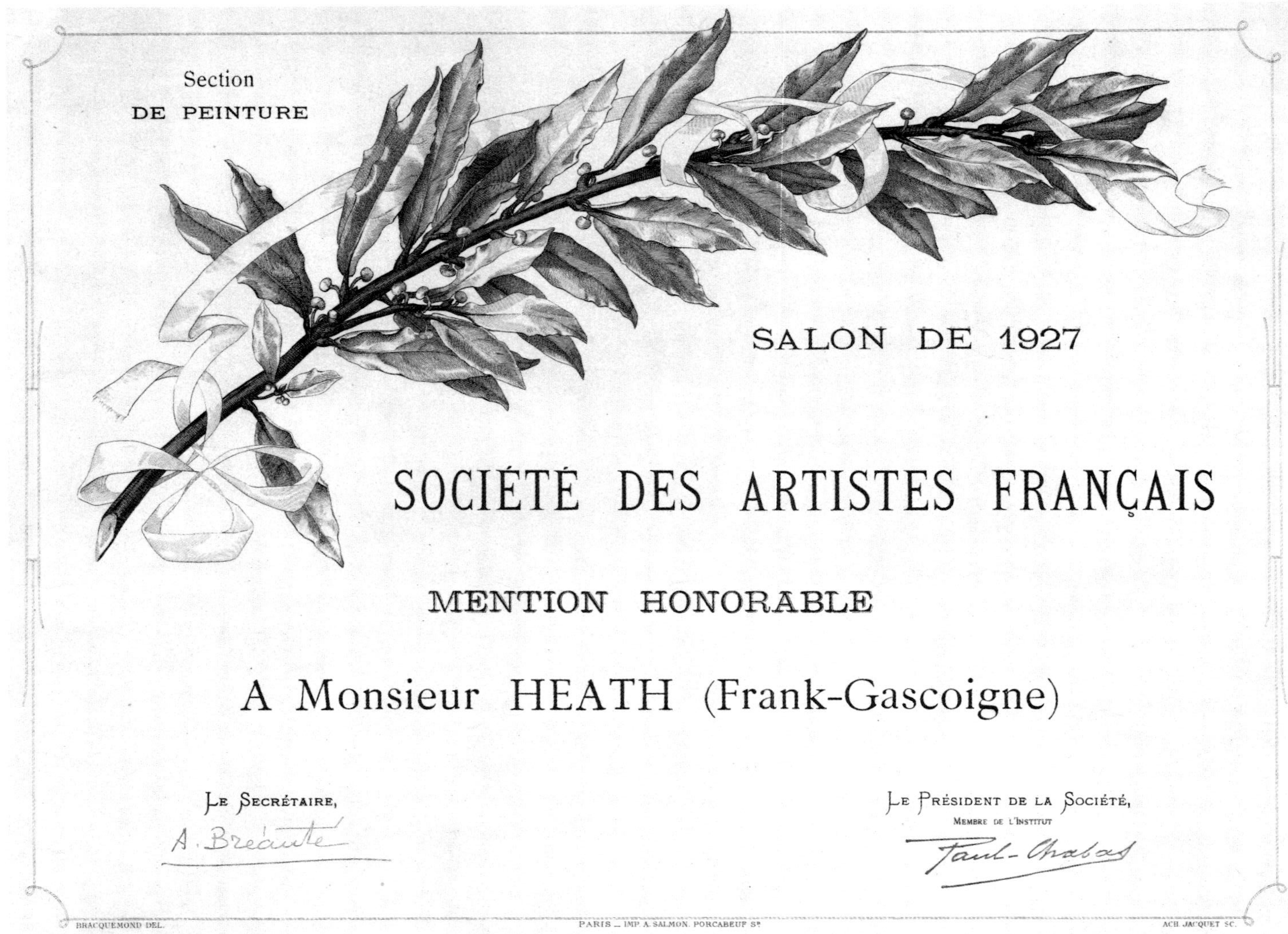

Chapter 5

HIS "NEWLYN SCHOOL" FRIENDS AT LAMORNA

In the early part of the century Lamorna must have been an idyllic place in which to live and paint. Its outstanding natural beauty, so varied, from the rolling countryside to the cliff and rock formations, made it a very attractive and scenic area for many artists. It was to this quiet valley that Frank Heath and his friends were drawn. Amongst his friends were:

Lamorna Birch (1869-1955)

One of the first to settle was Samuel John (Lamorna) Birch who, around 1890 aged 21, attracted by the fame of the "Newlyn School", set off for Cornwall from Manchester with £25 and his belongings in a tin trunk. On his first visit he found lodgings at Boleigh Farm (see Plate 13) at the head of the valley. Until 1895, Birch had been entirely self taught. In that year, however, on the advice of Stanhope Forbes, he went to study in Paris and on his return he based himself in Lamorna. His adoption of the name Lamorna was the result of confusion with another artist Lionel Birch. Not infrequently they got each other's mail and Stanhope Forbes finally settled matters by saying "We'll call you Lamorna Birch!"

In 1902 he received a letter signed E Haughton Vivian, asking for painting lessons. Unsure whether it was a man or woman, Birch addressed his reply "Dear Sir or Madam". He was, however, pleasantly surprised to discover that his pupil was an attractive young lady! Within a few months, Birch and "Mouse" as he called his new pupil were married and moved a mile down the valley to live in Flagstaff Cottage, formerly the harbour master's residence overlooking the cove (see page 20). Here their two daughters, Lamorna (Mornie) and Joan were born in 1904 and 1909 respectively. They all became great friends of the Heaths.

Lamorna Birch's work is permeated by his deep love of nature with some marvellous paintings of water and the various light effects and reflections to be achieved, especially on his beloved river at Lamorna. (See page 17)

Birch's output of both oils and watercolours was remarkably large; he was an excellent watercolourist (being made a full member of the Royal Society of Painters in Watercolours in 1914). He exhibited regularly at the Royal Academy and was made an RA in 1934.

He was a kind man who always found time and encouragement for the young painter. He spent several hours with Gabriel, Frank Heath's youngest daughter, on the banks of the Lamorna river teaching her about perspective and the patterns of light.

Dame Laura and Harold Knight

Laura Knight (1877-1970) was first introduced to Lamorna Birch soon after her arrival in Cornwall with her husband, Harold, in 1907; she was aged 30 and Harold 33. Initially they lived in Newlyn but in 1913 moved to Oakhill, a house at the head of the Lamorna

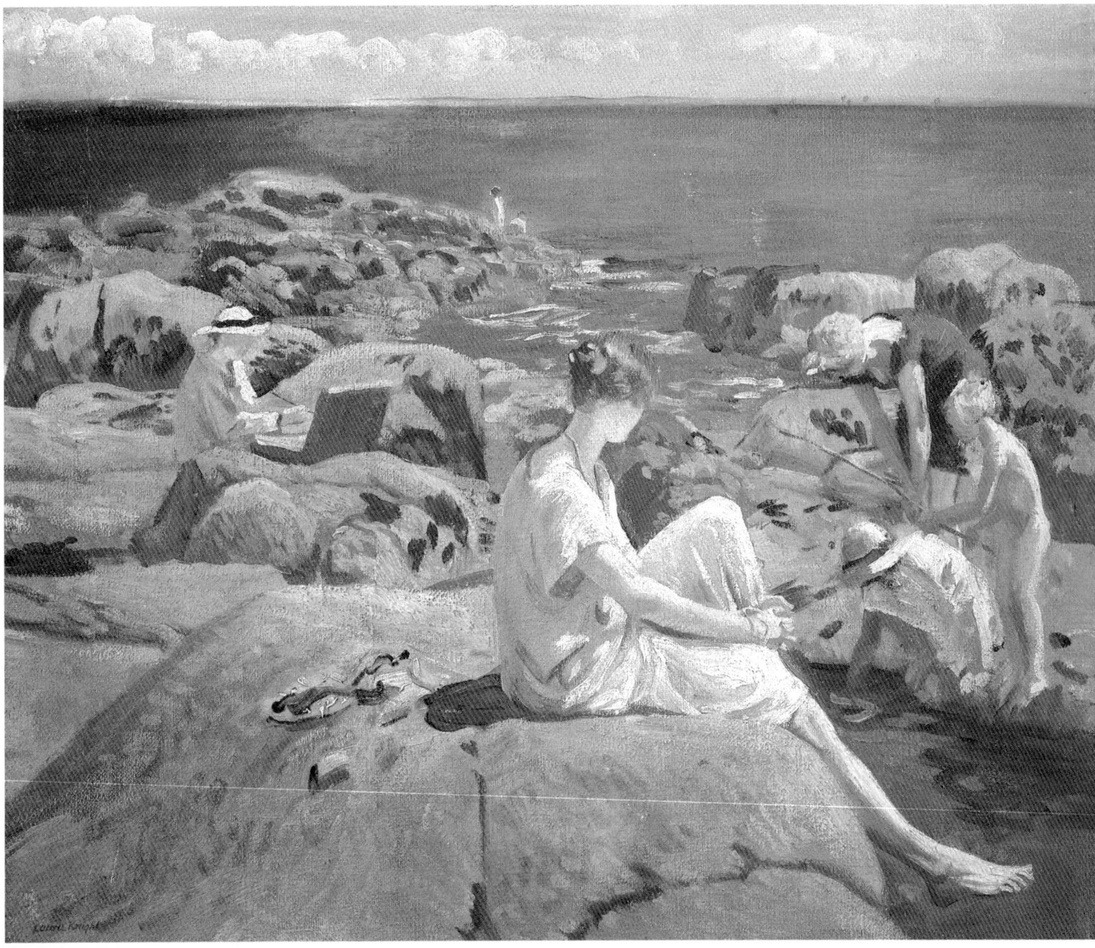

On the Rocks at Lamorna by Laura Knight

A picture of the Heath family. Jessica is painting, Nancy is in the foreground and Aileen, Tony and Gabriel are concentrating on their fishing.

valley which had been converted for them by Colonel Paynter, the local landowner, from a row of cottages. Colonel Paynter also built a large studio for them which was sited at the bottom of Frank Heath's garden at Menwinnion. The Colonel seems to have come to the rescue on other occasions. As the local landowner, he overruled local objections to Laura painting London models posing or swimming in the nude by the rocks. He also built her a hut on the cliffs near Carn Barges.

Laura spent over ten years of her life in Cornwall. Up to the outbreak of the War, it was a very happy period and this was reflected in her painting which became joyous and full of brilliant colour. As a result, she started to achieve wider recognition and success.

Harold (1874-1961) had a much quieter and reserved personality than Laura and tended to live in her shadow. He was, in many ways, the better artist of the two but never attained the same public renown as his wife. He was principally known for his portraits, and his painting of the characters at the Lamorna Inn (see page 23) is a good example of his work.

Harold and Laura moved to London at the end of the war; nevertheless, they kept studios at Lamorna for some years returning in the summers to paint. The picture opposite, painted by Laura in the early 1920s, shows the Heath family enjoying themselves on the rocks at Lamorna.

In London, Laura found a whole new range of subjects to paint starting with Diaghilev's ballets and the theatre in the 1920s and going on to the circus and gypsies over the following years. She was made a Dame of the British Empire in 1929 and became a Royal Academician in 1936. Harold was made a Royal Academician in 1937.

Sir Alfred Munnings (1878-1959)

Alfred Munnings ("AJ") arrived in Newlyn in 1908 aged 30 and made an immediate impact on the Forbes' students. He became the centre of an admiring crowd and was described by Laura Knight as "a young man with pale face and light brown hair combed forward who might have sat for a Robbie Burns portrait. His fine figure was clothed in a shepherd's plaid suit, the trousers were close fitting, belling out at the foot. .... never have I come across such overwhelming vitality. I could not take my eyes off him..... I adored everything about him. Harold, not so impulsive as I, stood aloof, withholding his judgement - fighting our new friend's charm". "AJ" boasted in later life that "he organized more parties, picnics, outings and Christmas festivities than anyone in the country" and certainly in Newlyn no congenial gathering was regarded as complete without him. Initially "AJ" lived in Newlyn and later moved to Lamorna where he lodged at the Lamorna Inn and rented a studio near to Lamorna Mill.

It was soon after his arrival in Newlyn that "AJ" met Florence Edith Carter-Wood, while she was visiting her brother Joey who was studying at the Forbes' School. She was tall, fair, blue eyed and most attractive and "AJ" did not take long to fall in love with her. They were married in January 1912 and whilst on their honeymoon in London, Florence tried to commit suicide by taking cyanide due to a depressive illness. She recovered and was hurried back to Lamorna where they lived at Cliff House (now the Lamorna Cove Hotel). The marriage was never a happy one and "AJ" retreated into his bachelor lifestyle - going off painting for days at a time, leaving the often depressed Florence to her own devices and the support of the sociable group of painters. Amongst these was Jessica Heath who became a great friend and support.

On 23 July 1914, during a fancy dress party at Trewarveneth, the lodgings of Geoffrey Garnier, Florence, following verbal abuse from "AJ" returned to Cliff House. After breakfast the next morning she went to their bedroom and again took cyanide and died soon afterwards. She was 25 years of age and her grave is marked by a simple granite stone in the nearby churchyard of Sancreed. Jessica was greatly affected by this tragic event, relating that "a shadow had come over the Valley".

After Florence's death, "AJ" spent less and less time at Lamorna. Following the outbreak of the First World War, he was determined to enlist (despite having lost the sight of one eye in an accident when he was 21) and eventually found a job training army horses; later he was to go as an official war artist to France. He stayed with Frank and Jessica Heath at Menwinnion on several occasions during the early part of the war. While at Lamorna he was known locally as "the man who could really paint a horse" and it was for this subject that he became famous.

Throughout his life, "A.J." loved writing ballads and poems mainly with a horsy flavour and it was while staying with the Heaths in 1915 that he was inspired to write his famous ballad – "The Tale of Anthony Bell", a hunting story in sixty verses. In the introductory verse he was baffled to think of a word that would rhyme with "foxes" and it was only when returning one day on his horse up Rocky Lane to Menwinnion that he hit upon "boxes". Having achieved this, he was quickly into his stride to complete this long ballad.

> Now, Anthony Bell, of whom I tell,
> Was always hunting foxes,
> He lived at a place called Highfield Hall,
> His horses were standing in every stall;
> There were horses in all the boxes...

First verse of The Tale of Anthony Bell

This party piece which he related at many notable functions in future years was first performed at a Lamorna Christmas celebration in 1915. During that same Christmas while at Menwinnion, "A.J." painted the portrait of Anthony Bell which was one of several sketches illustrating this tale; these pictures were created to decorate the walls of Aileen and Nancy's doll's house. (See page 33.)

After the war, he bought Castle House at Dedham and married again. He became a Royal Academician in 1926 and President of the RA in 1944; he was knighted the same year.

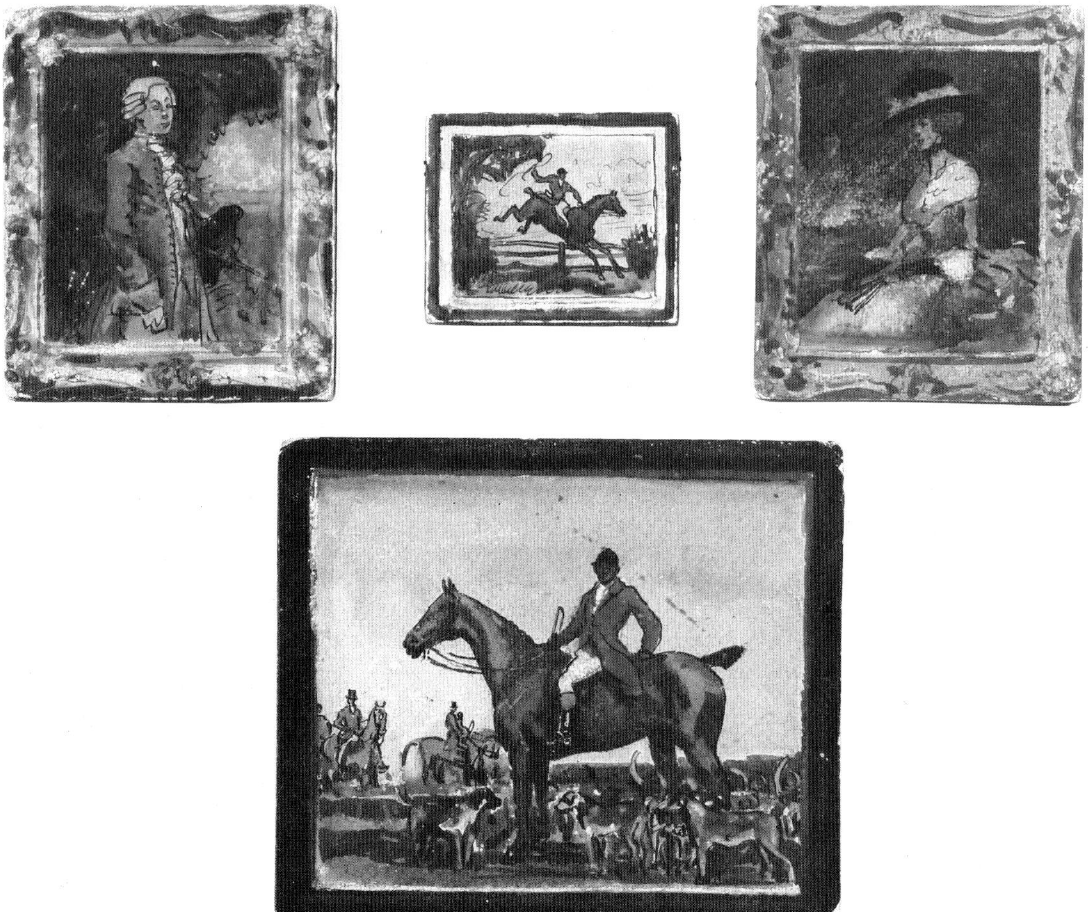

Pictures from the doll's house

Charles Simpson (1885-1971)

Charles Simpson was a self-taught artist, apart from a short period studying under Lucy Kemp-Welch, the animal painter, at her School of Painting in Bushey. Perhaps in order to learn more about painting horses, he then worked with Munnings in Norfolk during the early 1900s. This was the beginning of a lifelong friendship with Munnings and it may have been Charles who encouraged Munnings to visit Cornwall.

Charles himself came to Cornwall in 1905, aged 20, attracted by the presence of other artists and by the landscape. He took lessons in landscape painting from the St Ives artist, J Noble Barlow, who used to paint sometimes at Lamorna in a similar manner to Lamorna Birch. Charles took a studio in Newlyn and it was while working there that he met his

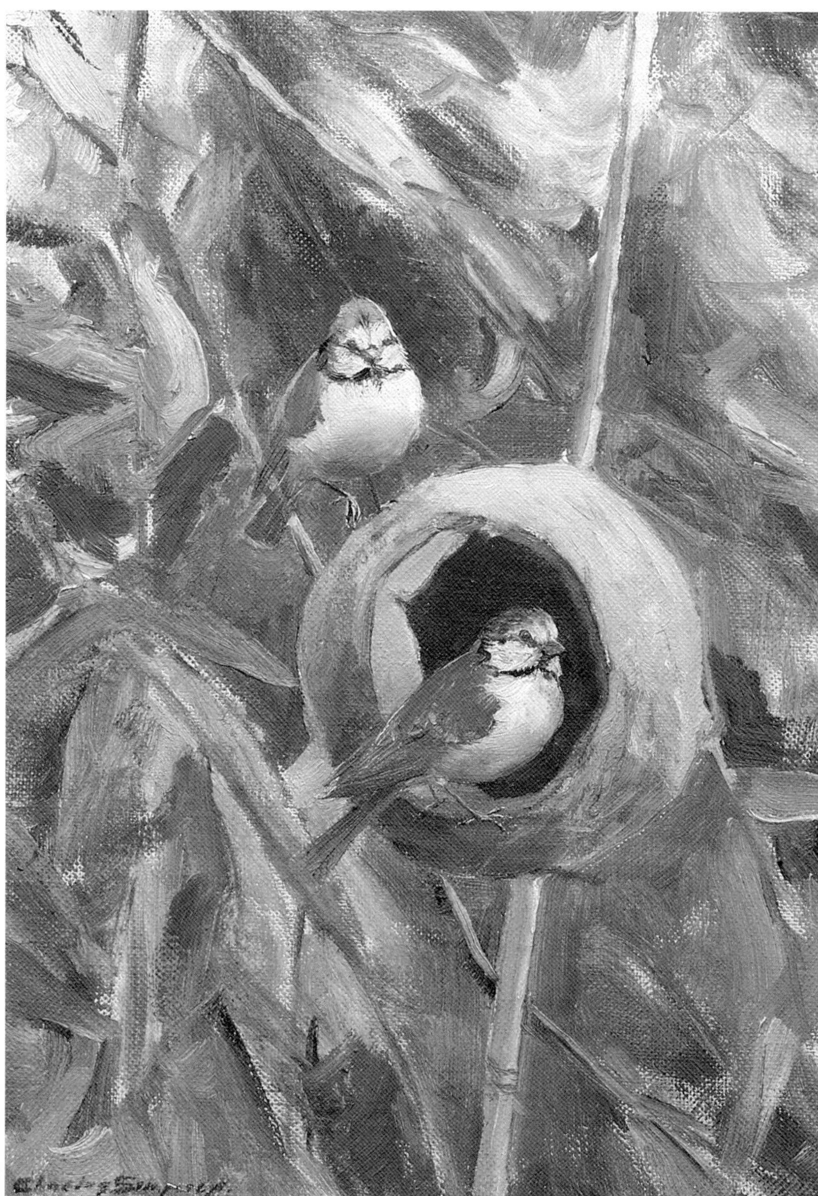

Blue Tits by Charles Simpson

future wife, Ruth Alison, while she was studying at the Forbes' School. They were married in 1913 and lived in Newlyn where their daughter Leonora was born. In 1916 they moved to St Ives where they ran a painting school from 1920-1924. During his time in Newlyn and St Ives, Charles painted animal, bird and landscape subjects.

However in 1924, perhaps as a desire for either a change or greater financial security, the family moved to London. Here, great success came to him in the way of commissions, mainly of hunting scenes and race meetings. In 1931, the family returned to Cornwall and lived in "Duncans" at Lamorna. This house commanded a beautiful position overlooking the cove, being situated higher up the cliffs, above Lamorna Birch's home at Flagstaff Cottage. It was from here that he was able to continue to paint the landscape that had always attracted him. He moved to Penzance in 1946.

Charles Simpson's range of subjects was extensive and his work was exhibited at the Royal Academy and many Galleries.

Robert (Bertie) and Eleanor Hughes

Bertie Hughes (1873-1953) and Eleanor Waymouth (1882-1959) both came to Newlyn to study at the Forbes' School; they fell in love and were married at St Buryan Church in 1910. In 1912, "Chyangwheal" was built for them (at the top of the valley on the road to Boleigh) and they lived there for the rest of their lives. They were close friends of the Heaths.

Bertie Hughes spent most of his life painting the landscape around Lamorna. He is remembered for regular habits. Every morning, he would set off and find somewhere

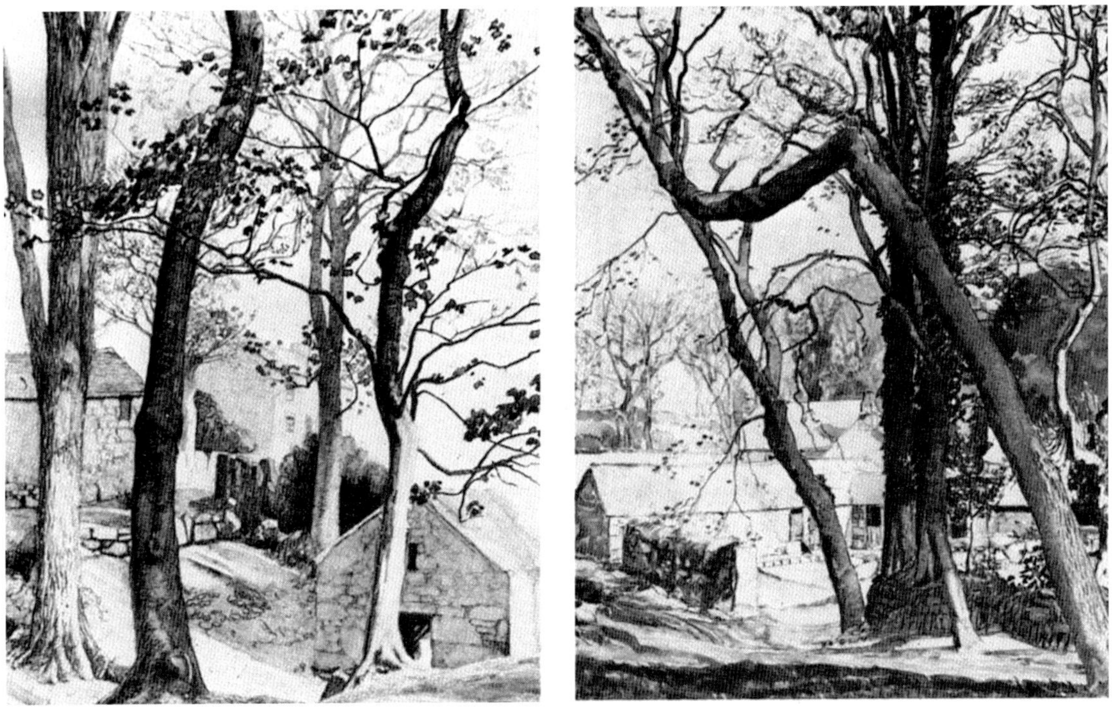

Trewoofe Farm by Eleanor Hughes

comfortable to paint and every lunchtime he was to be found at the Lamorna Inn having a drink and playing the card game, euchre.

Much of Eleanor's work was in watercolour and depicted the countryside which she loved. The pictures opposite show farm buildings at Trewoofe. The farm at Trewoofe provided great scope for the Lamorna artists and was painted frequently: see also Frank Heath's "The Road to the Farm". (Plate 32)

Both Bertie and Eleanor Hughes exhibited at the Royal Academy from 1910.

In the same lane as Chyangwheal was "Rosemerrin", the home of the artist, Benje Leader who was killed in the First World War and later, the writer, Crosbie Garstin, the son of Norman Garstin (one of the early Newlyn artists). Mrs Crosbie Garstin was the principal first violin in the Penzance Orchestral Society of which Frank Heath was also a member. (See page 91.)

Charles and Ella Naper

In 1913, Charles (1882-1968) and Ella (1886-1972) Naper built themselves Trewoofe House (at the top of the valley) where they lived for the rest of their lives. Charles briefly studied architecture before going to the Royal Academy Schools. He was principally a landscape painter and, in particular, spent much time, executing detailed studies of the rock formations near Land's End. He exhibited at the Royal Academy between 1910 and 1933.

Ella worked from home producing decorative enamel and horn work jewellery. She designed a memorial to Benje Leader in St Buryan Church. Both Charles and Ella were keen gardeners and they created a lovely garden at Trewoofe. The Napers were great friends with the Knights and Laura used Ella as her model on many occasions.

The writer, Mrs Alfred Sidgwick lived nearby at Trewoofe Orchard where Frank Heath would visit to play chess with her husband, an Oxford Professor.

Stanley Gardiner (1888-1952)

Another artist to settle in Lamorna, was Stanley Gardiner. In the early 1920s, while on a painting holiday in the area, he met Lamorna Birch who told him of a cottage to let in the valley. There he built his studio and frame making shop. In order to augment his income from painting, he made picture frames for many local artists (including Stanhope Forbes). Eventually achieving success with his painting, he exhibited widely, showing at the Royal Academy between 1927-1947. He specialized in landscapes and flower studies, mainly in oils, but was also an accomplished watercolourist. He lived at Lily Cottage, overlooking the river.

Chapter 6

THE POST WAR YEARS

Frank Heath was by nature modest and easy going and the post war years were an increasingly difficult time for him as a family man on a small income. He did not make a living from his art, lacking the promotional flair of Lamorna Birch or AJ Munnings. His declining health, following the attack of meningitis in 1915, which had left him lacking in energy and willpower, was largely to blame. Few realized how he had suffered, not least those who knew little of his moods and depressions. At times these were all pervasive and left him sullen and uncommunicative.

What is so interesting is that his pictures did not reflect his difficulties, rather the reverse. Certainly it was in the 1920s that he became renowned for his feeling for colour and light and their effective depiction on canvas. During this period he produced some of his best paintings and had his greatest successes at exhibitions. From 1927-1930, he had 6 works accepted by the Salon in Paris and his picture of Mousehole Harbour (Plate 16) received a "Mention Honorable" in their 1927 exhibition. (See page 72.)

He also exhibited at the Royal Academy, where his picture of The Butterfly (Plate 20) was hung "on the line" in 1928, and the Walker Art Gallery in Liverpool. However, it was at the Newlyn Art Gallery, in the company of his many friends of the second generation of Newlyn artists - from Lamorna (Lamorna Birch, Bertie and Eleanor Hughes, "Seal" Weatherby, Charles Naper and Stanley Gardiner) and Newlyn (Stanhope Forbes, Ernest and Dod Proctor, Thomas Cooper Gotch, Norman Garstin, Geoffrey and Jill Garnier and Harold Harvey), that the majority of Frank Heath's fine paintings were shown in the 1920/30s. Set out below is a list of these paintings together with the reviews, made at the time, extracted from "The Cornishman".

1921

The Trapper.... "a picture which instantly claims attention. The central figure, a sturdy trapper, advancing up a well known Cornish cliff path, with firm swinging stride, bearing a string of rabbits on his shoulder, is strongly drawn. A boy is holding open a gate through which the man passes. In the background one gets a glimpse of a turbulent March sea with a couple of steam drifters bruising their way westwards to the fishing grounds. The combined effect is charming in the extreme."

Feeding Pigs.... "a typical west country scene."

Boleigh Farm.... "a quaint homestead, near St Buryan." (Plate 13)

Washing Day.... "two women engaged in washing clothes. The figures are admirably drawn and the treatment of the lighting effects is most successful."

1922 "A trio of most arresting pictures by Mr F G Heath."

Summer Morning.... "Mr Heath depicts with great skill the bold headland and the rocks at the base warmed by the soft morning sun. A group of children who have been bathing in the pool in the foreground gives it a touch of life and the blue of the pool and a peep of the sea beyond add to the charm of the colouring."

Saturday Morning in Harbour.... "a canvas crowded with fishing boats strongly drawn, the suppressed treatment of the houses along the shore adding power by contrast to the foreground." (Plate 16)

"There is music in the night".... "if 'Saturday Morning in Harbour' might be taken as symbolising the commercial spirit of the place, this picture might symbolise its mysticism. The scene is that chosen for 'Summer Morning' but the treatment is totally different. The moon, hidden behind light clouds, sheds a subdued light on the spray from the headland and on the broken water rushing from the rocks at the base. It is full of the poetry of beauty." (Plate 15)

1923

The Approach of Night. The Wolf.... "Nothing more impressive from the point of view of ponderous strength has been seen in the gallery for a long time. The artist depicts a stretch of coast line towards Land's End. On the left foreground, the rocks stand up almost perpendicularly in rugged masses. On the otherside there is a sweep of the coast and the tops of the cliffs are tinged with the setting sun. In the immediate foreground the sea comes into a little bay, Away on the horizon is a tiny speck of light - the Wolf Rock Lighthouse. The sun has gone down behind a bank of cloud which is permeated by its glow."

Last Day of the Holidays.... "is also an outstanding work. The scene is of Lamorna where a group of young people is assembled. The principal figure is that of a young girl, who is leaning listlessly in a boat, looking out across the sea as if regretting the impending departure. The figures are excellently drawn and the grouping most attractive." (Plate 17)

The Little Maid.... "a study of a girl carrying a tray. Behind her is a window through which bright sun pours in. This work is beautifully conceived and executed and has called forth warm comment in well informed circles." (Plate 21)

1924 "Mr F G Heath revels in depicting sunlit scenes."

The Fairy Story.... "is a clever and delightful portrayal of dancing golden light beneath the trees; the look of intense interest on the faces of the 3 children as their elder companion reads to them from the crotch of a tree spells no small study of child character on the part of the artist." (Plate 19)

"Sunlight again permeates "The Tracing" and "Homework" as it streams through the window and reflects from the interior of the room."

1925

Fir Trees.... "The sunshine artist tries his hand at shade and the result is that of suppressed laughter on a happy young face, as the sun breaks through over the distant fields, although the immediate foreground has as much greyness as Mr Heath's love of sunlight would allow him to use."

Maidenhood.... "The full, warm summer sun of late morning streams down the staircase to the girl's figure in the quaint, old- fashioned cream-coloured dress; downstairs the light comes flowing from the opened windows of the ground-floor rooms. The effect is marvellously carried out."

1926

"Mr Heath is rather concentrating on etchings, of which he has 4. They are clever and pleasing but there is not the delightful individuality in them that one always sees smiling from his sun bathed oils which have very often been the salt of the Newlyn exhibitions."

1927

Fishing for Grey Mullet from the Rocks.... "is a large work, with a suggestion of the near presence of sunlight, without its being actually a visible feature. But we do get light, thrown back from the rocks in the background, and from the brilliant silver of the fish at the feet of the men in the foreground; a very refreshing and restful picture".

1927 (continued)

The Store Pot.... "the rowing boat pulls us out to the swell off the coast and the rower rests on his oars, as the man in the bow poises the store-pot on the edge of the boat. There is rich colour in this sea-study." (Plate 26)

1928

The Butterfly.... "is of a girl wrapped in a bath towel, seated on the edge of her bath; on her knee is a white butterfly and her face, downcast as she looks at the insect, is warm with the glow of sunlight which encircles it as it streams in at the window." (Plate 20)

The Cretonne Chair.... "a brilliant colour study."

Fishing Harbour at low tide.

1929 "Mr Heath has never presented anything more attractive and beautiful than the three paintings he has on view."

The Model.... "is a nude girl just in early adolescence sitting with her back to the spectator in front of an upper window. Round her are ranged different coloured balloons. The pose of the girl is graceful, natural: the drawing and the colour bring out the beauty of the youthful human figure while the light on the balloons is exceedingly well done."

Girl and Parrot.... "is a delightful piece of colouring." (Plate 22)

The Green Dress.

1930

Girl Cleaning Kettle.... "Mr F G Heath has a delightful work, alike in its conception and treatment. It is instinct with colour, suffused with sunshine and there is a delicacy of touch which is captivating. The title does not do it justice."

Madonna Lilies.... "a mass of lilies against a background of open countryside." (Cover and Plate 24)

Butterflies in Buddleia.

1933

The Hillside.... "full of clouds and the beauty of wild countryside."

1934

White Ducks at Lamorna Mill. (Plate 30)

Girl Knitting and The Letter.... "2 figure studies"

1935

The Problem.... "a girl deep in thought over her next chess move."

The Road to the farm. (Plate 32)

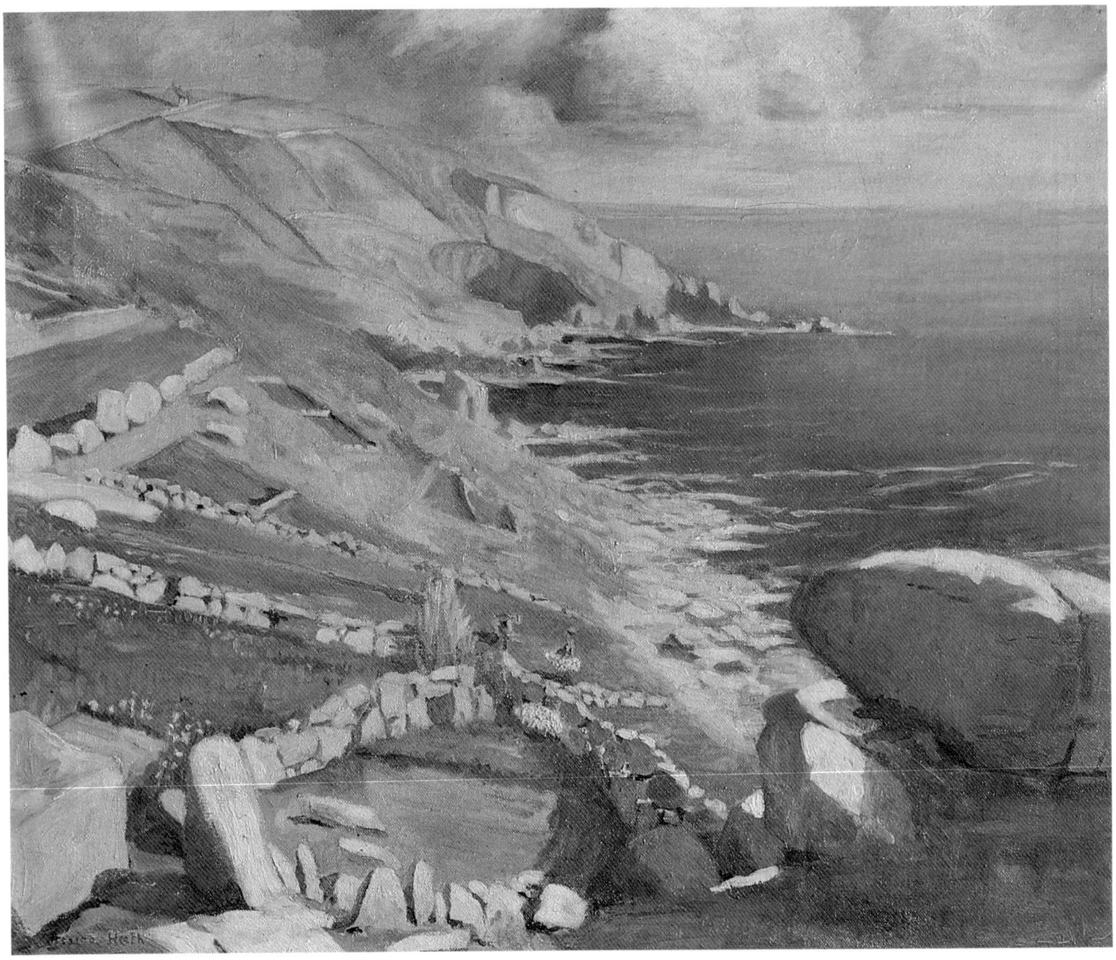

The view from Carn Barges, looking east towards Carn Du
by Jessica Heath

At the time of this painting, the land on the cliff was cultivated and all the meadows were worked by the Ladner family of Perch; they grew daffodils and early potatoes. (All this land now has reverted back to scrub.)

When not painting, Frank's life revolved around his family and his various interests. Jessica was very much the centre of the family with her strong will, energy and self-reliance. She was always busy - whether it be looking after the children, including the making of the majority of their clothes or tending their large garden. When she had some spare time, she enjoyed painting the local landscape and, in particular, the coastline around Lamorna.

The family lived simply and made their own entertainment, exploring and enjoying the countryside and coast around Menwinnion. In the summer, many hours were spent swimming in the sea, picnicing and playing on the rocks below Carn Barges - about 2 miles walk from Menwinnion. Roller skating was also a popular pastime, especially on the main road to St Buryan which had been recently tarmaced.

The Heaths had several pets to look after. Jock, the terrier; Tim, the labrador; Cronje, the donkey; Silko, the cat, not to mention rabbits and a tortoise.

Jock was a menace. He had a brother owned by John Collins (a gardener employed by Mrs Paynter at Boskenna) who lived at the cove. They had a reputation of being the worst

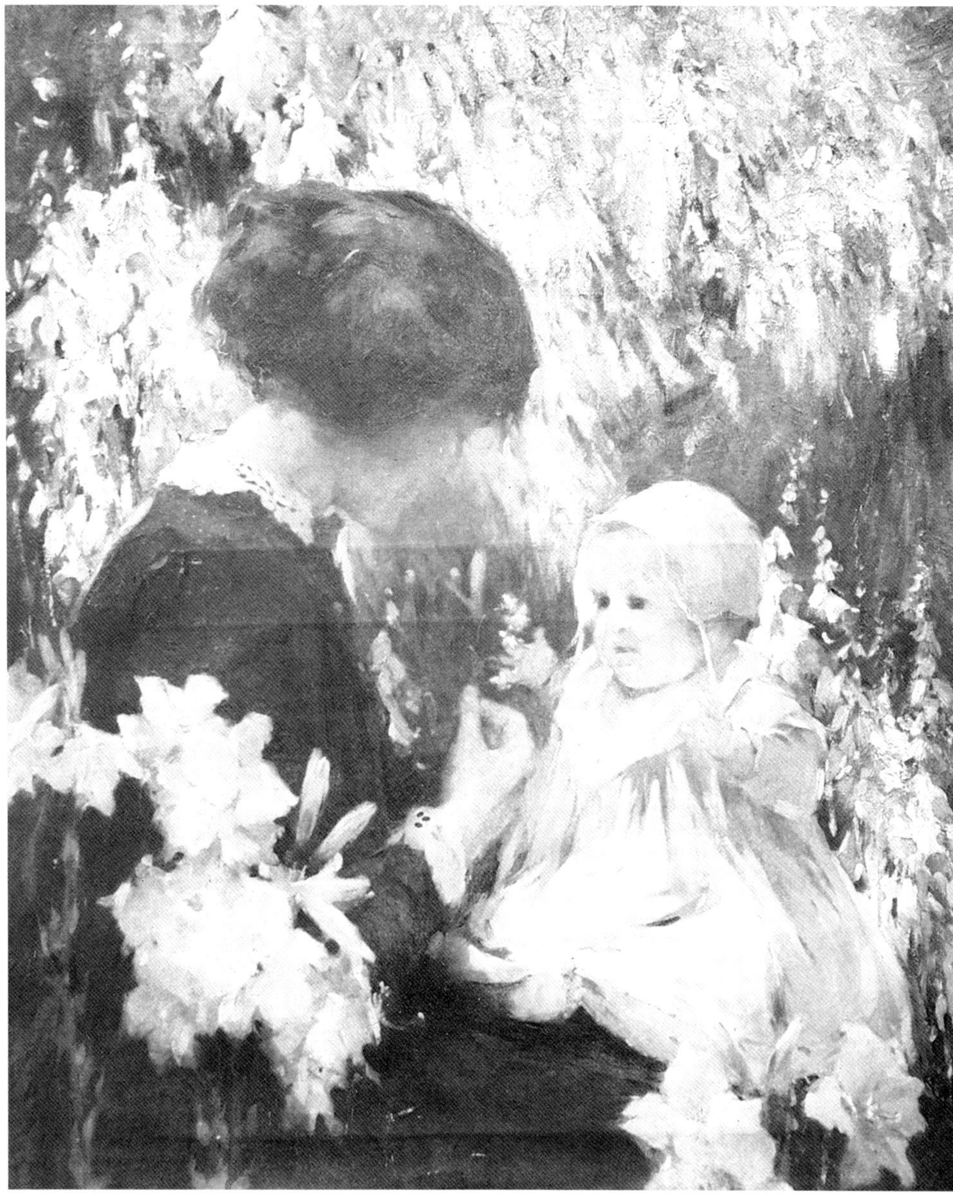

Jessica in "Mother and Child"
by Frank Heath. Oil 40" x 32"
Exhibited at the Royal Academy in 1913

dogs in the parish. (This was confirmed by a recent churchwarden at St Buryan who remembers when walking to church as a boy, having to make a long detour to avoid Rocky Lane and the entrance to Menwinnion and the attentions of Jock.)

In the mid 1920s, Frank bought his first car, an Austin, which was used principally to ferry the children to and from school in Penzance. Up until then, Aileen, who was a weekly boarder at St Clare's, was taken and collected by her mother on Monday mornings and Friday afternoons. They used the same bicycle which they took in turns to ride. The 5 mile journey from school to Menwinnion must have been hard work as it included the formidable climb up Paul Hill. Later on Nancy followed Aileen to St Clare's, while for their early education, Tony and Gabriel shared a governess, Miss Stone who came by bicycle from St Buryan. Gabriel then followed her sisters to St Clare's while Tony went first to prep school at St Erbyn's before going on to Clifton College.

The car, which was christened "Old Henry" by the family, also enabled Frank, Jessica

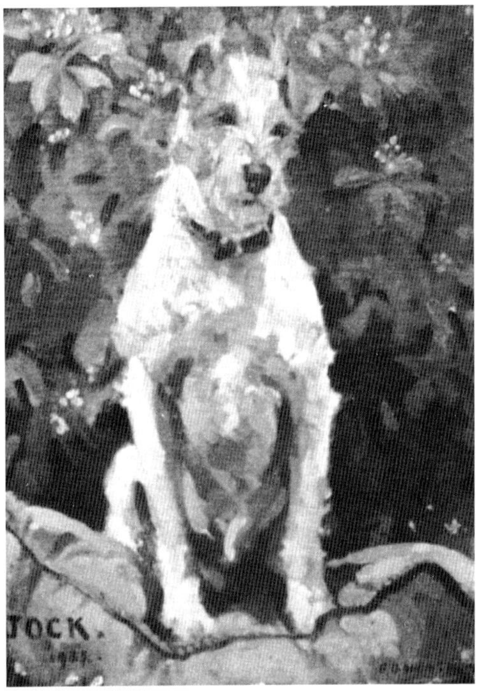

Jock

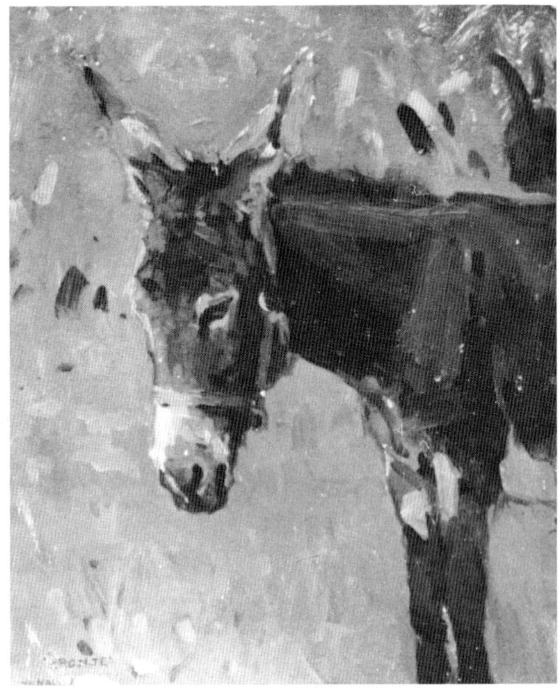

Cronje

and their children to travel further afield for holidays and outings. Several annual holidays were spent at Porthminster Beach, near St Ives (Plate 28) where the family must have enjoyed the contrast of sand under their feet to the rocks at Lamorna.

In 1925, Frank and Jessica took a few days holiday in North Devon with "Old Henry" in order to watch the British Amateur Golf Championship being played that year at Westward Ho! The letter opposite, written by Frank to Aileen, gives some of his impressions on the golfing fashions of the day.

Frank was a very keen sportsman who played both golf and cricket. He and the family enjoyed playing golf together, both at the Penzance Golf Club at Sancreed, and at the West Cornwall Golf Club at Lelant, near St Ives. The "Cornishman" makes mention of their successes in various competitions, especially Aileen, who, at the age of 14 and for the next two years, won the Cornwall Girls championship for which she was presented with the Bolitho Rose Bowl.

Frank's other great interest was music. He was an accomplished violinist and played for many years as a second violin with the Penzance Orchestral Society. The picture on page 90 shows the Orchestra during a concert given at St John's Hall, Penzance in the early 1930s. (Walter Barnes is the conductor and Frank Heath is sitting in the second seat of the front row on the right hand side.) The Society was founded in 1906 by Walter Barnes who became its first and long serving conductor.

Frank's painting studio also had another use - that of music rehearsal room and he would spend many hours practising his violin there. Making music was a very popular pastime and he played in a small chamber music group at Menwinnion and other artists' homes; both Stanhope Forbes and Charles Simpson were keen musicians.

Frank Heath's impressions of the golfing fashions of the day.

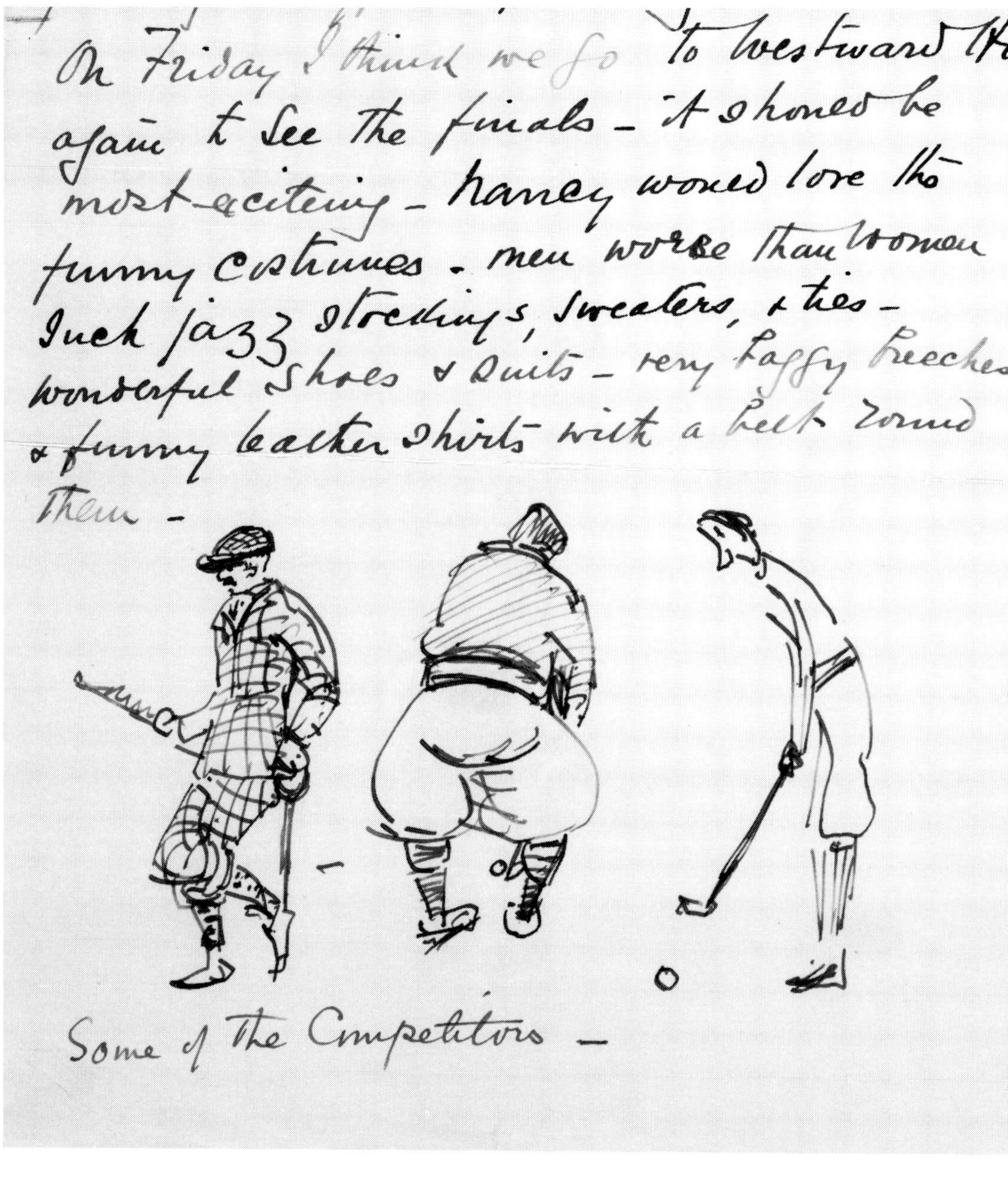
On Friday I think we go to Westward Ho
again to see the finals - it should be
most exciting - Nancy would love the
funny costumes - men worse than women
such jazz stockings, sweaters, & ties -
wonderful shoes & suits - very baggy breeches
& funny leather shirts with a belt round
them -

Some of the Competitors -

The Penzance Orchestral Society

The Orchestra during a concert given at St. John's Hall, Penzance in the early 1930s.
(Frank Heath is sitting in the second seat of the front row on the right hand side.)

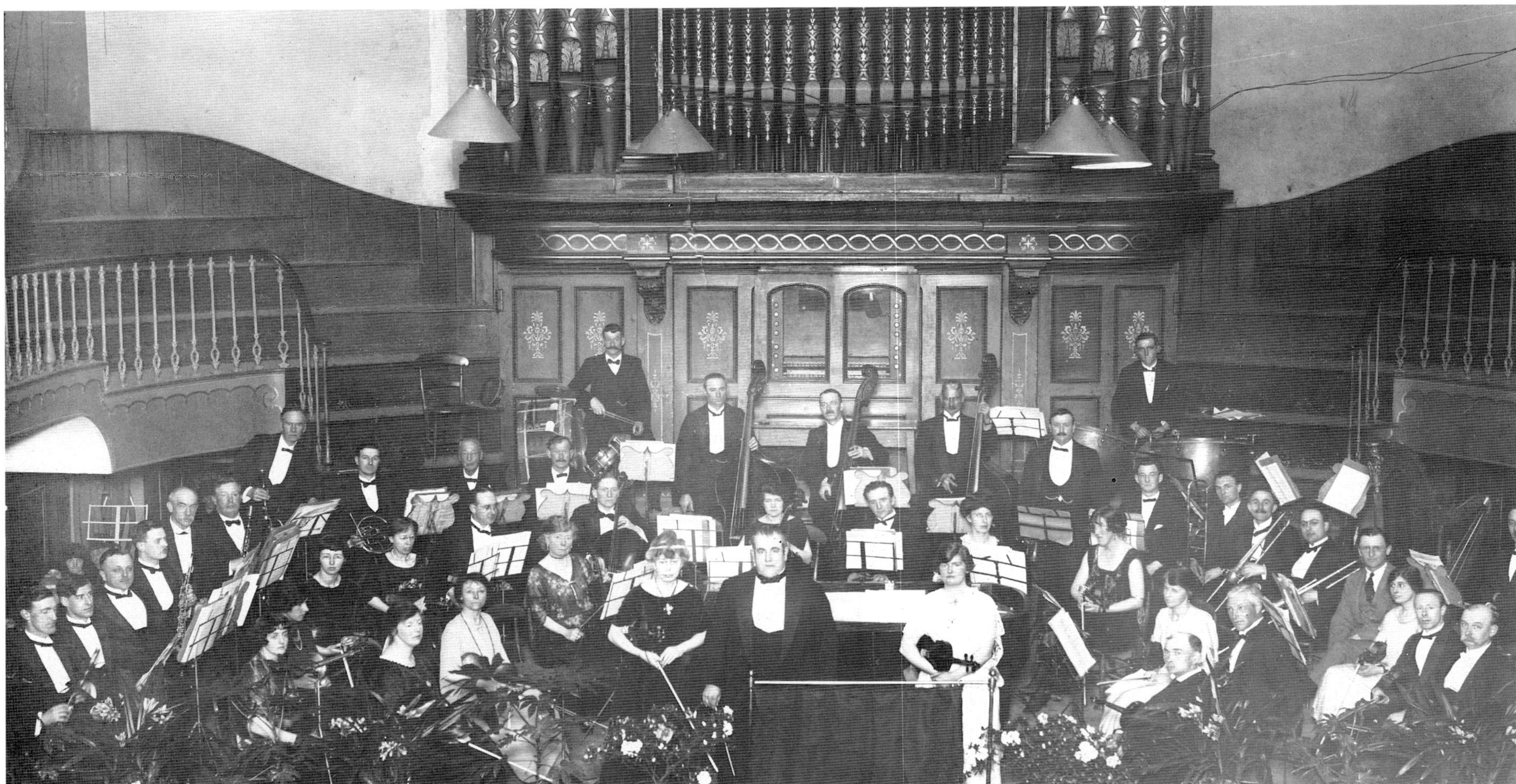

The Penzance Orchestral Society

A list of the members of the Orchestra at a concert given at St John's Hall, Penzance in November 1931

ORCHESTRA

First Violins—

Mrs. Crosbie Garstin (Principal)
Miss W. Beadsworth
,, Kathleen Paul
,, Margery Holden
,, Rowenna Maddern
,, Williams
Mr. George Beadsworth
,, Kenneth Woolcock
,, Frank Tamblyn
,, M. Cocking
,, Stuart Thompson

Second Violins—

Mr. A. W, Firth (Principal)
,, Frank G. Heath
Miss Kathleen Frazier
,, D. Stone
,, Lilian Tonkin
,, Dorothy Toy
Mr. Huntingford
,, Morgan Hosking
,, Norman Truman
,, F. B. Grose
,, G. Cave-Day

Violas—

Mr. Barrie Bennetts (Principal)
Mrs. W. N. Main
Miss Carling
Mrs Dudley Harris
Miss Marjorie Vercoe
Mrs. William Lloyd

Violoncellos—

Mr, R. A. Hoskins (Principal)
Miss Monica Arthur-West
,, Baldrey
Mr. Roy Thompson
,, Herbert Luke
,, W. H, Hallward
,, Vivian Thomas
,, White
,, E. J. Chapple

Contra Basses—

Mr. G. Howard White (Principal)
,, W. E. Williams
Major H. Sainsbury
Mr. N. Tregarthen
,, E. Arthur-West

Flutes—

Mr. F. N. Hodson
,, Wm. Lloyd
,, A. E. Lewin

Piccolo—

Mr A. E. Lewin

Oboes—

Mr. A. Brien
,, G. L. Bradley

Clarinets—

Mr. George Laurance
,, V. Ursell

Bassoons—

Mr. W, Piper
,, F. Latham

Horns—

Mr. W, Parsons
,, Willmett
,, W. E. Oates
,, W. Moon

Trumpets—

Mr. Eric Ball
,, T. McGuinness

Trombones—

Mr. W. B. Prowse
,, J. H, Gillis
,, Herbert Kessell
,, Chas. H, Roach

Tuba—

Mr. J. Probert

Tympani—

Mr, L. Stewart

Harp—

Mr. A. W. Robinson

Percussion—

Mr Bernard Beardmore

Hon. Conductor :—WALTER BARNES

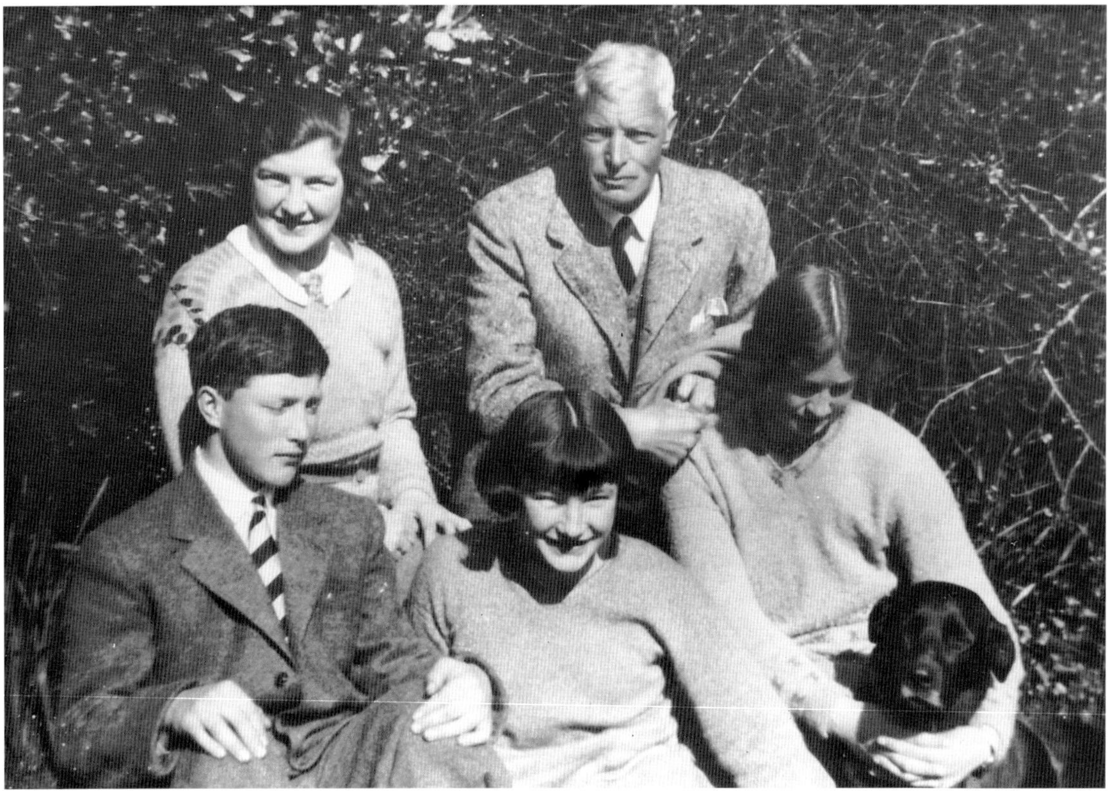

Frank Heath with his children (circa 1930)

The four children were growing up fast. Aileen had moved up to London to study physiotherapy at St Thomas's Hospital and Queen Mary's, Carshalton. Nancy remained at home while Tony, after Clifton College went on to Gonville and Caius College, Cambridge where he gained his rugby blue. He played for Penzance and Rosslyn Park and had a trial for England. He also played cricket for Cornwall. Gabriel continued at St Clare's School until she transferred to Ingleside, a boarding school at Budleigh Salterton in Devon.

During this time Frank Heath's health gradually worsened and in 1935 he collapsed at Menwinnion with breathing problems. After treatment in hospital at Penzance he returned home to convalesce but his condition did not improve. At that time Aileen was working for a specialist in London and it was decided to seek his advice. It was therefore early in 1936 that Frank travelled up to London by train to be admitted to a nursing home in Wimpole Street. Although making a slight recovery at first, he died peacefully in June of that year.

The funeral was held at Old Coulsdon Church, Surrey and he was buried in the family grave in accordance with his father's wishes - that the oldest and youngest of his 12 children should be buried with him and their mother.

Subsequently a teak seat was placed in the churchyard on which the names of William Heath, his wife and their 12 children are remembered. (See page 8.)

POSTSCRIPTS

The Past

After Frank Heath's death, Jessica decided to leave Menwinnion and moved to Frome Cottage at Frampton in Dorset. The house was sold to John and Nicky Williams, the brothers of the Cornish author, "Elephant Bill" Williams; "Elephant Bill" himself moved into the house after the Second World War. Subsequently, Menwinnion became a country house hotel before, more recently, being acquired and extended for use as a home for the elderly.

In 1942, Jessica returned "to her roots" at Bandon in Co Cork, before finally settling, 10 years later, in the country at Shippool, Innishannon, Co Cork. She died in 1967, aged 83.

The Present

Frank Heath's youngest daughter, Gabriel, is a very accomplished painter both in oils and watercolours and has had several pictures exhibited at the Royal Academy. This year she celebrates her 80th birthday.

The Future

One of Frank Heath's great grandsons, Orlando Seale has inherited the family's artistic talent. Also born a few months ago, Nicolas Tony Heath, the first great grandson of Frank who will carry on the family name of Heath.

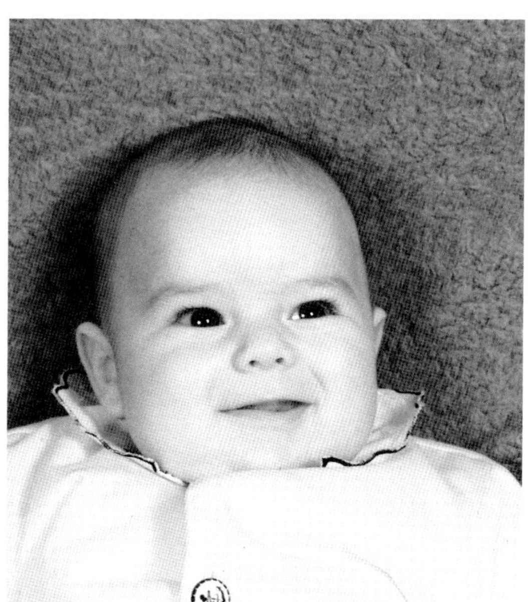

Nicolas Tony Heath, born July 1994

Photographic Acknowledgements:

I would like to thank the undermentioned for the courtesy of allowing me to reproduce the following pictures in this book. (Every effort has been made to contact the copyright holders.)

Colour:

Royal Cornwall Museum, Truro (Plate 7)

Galerie Dobiaschofsky, Berne, Switzerland (Plate 23)

Richard Green, London (Plates 5, 17, 18)

The Medici Society Ltd (Plates 10, 24, 25, 30, 31)

David Messum Fine Art (Plate 2)

Phillips Fine Art Auctioneers, London (Plates 6, 13, 15, 28)

The Directors of the Queens Hotel, Penzance (Plate 26)

Black and White:

Copyright British Library (Page 11)

City of Aberdeen Art Gallery and Museums Collections (Page 13)

Ferens Art Gallery, Hull City Museums, Art Galleries and Archives (Page 14)

Haynes Fine Art (Page 23)

Neales, Nottingham (Page 6)

Phillips Fine Art Auctioneers, London (Pages 17 and 76)

Penzance and District Museum and Art Gallery (Page 78)

Copyright Augustus John, by permission of the Estate of the late Vivien White (Page 25)

Copyright Dame Laura Knight, by permission of the Curtis Brown Group Ltd, London (Pages 23 and 74)